To my husband Jon, who is my everything, and also who
helped me come up with the title of this book

—*J. S.*

Published by
Peachtree Publishing Company Inc.
1700 Chattahoochee Avenue
Atlanta, Georgia 30318-2112
*www.peachtree-online.com*

Text © 2019 by Jennifer Swanson
Illustrations © 2019 by TeMika Grooms

The illustrations were rendered digitally.

Edited by Kathy Landwehr
Design and composition by Nicola Simmonds Carmack
Diagrams by Adela Pons

Printed in June 2019 by RR Donnelley in China
10 9 8 7 6 5 4 3 2 1
First Edition
ISBN 978-1-68263-022-8

Library of Congress Cataloging-in-Publication Data

Names: Swanson, Jennifer, author. | Grooms, TeMika, illustrator.
Title: Save the crash-test dummies / written by Jennifer Swanson ; illustrated by TeMika Grooms.
Description: Atlanta : Peachtree Publishing Company Inc., [2019] | Audience: Ages 8–12. | Audience:
Grades 4 to 6. | Includes bibliographical references and index.
Identifiers: LCCN 2019017782 | ISBN 9781682630228
Subjects: LCSH: Automobiles—Safety measures—History—Juvenile literature. | Automobiles—
Crashworthiness—History—Juvenile literature. | Automobiles—Design and construction—History—
Juvenile literature.
Classification: LCC TL242 .S925 2019 | DDC 629.2/76—dc23 LC record available at
*https://lccn.loc.gov/2019017782*

# Save the Crash-test Dummies

**Jennifer Swanson**

**Illustrated by TeMika Grooms**

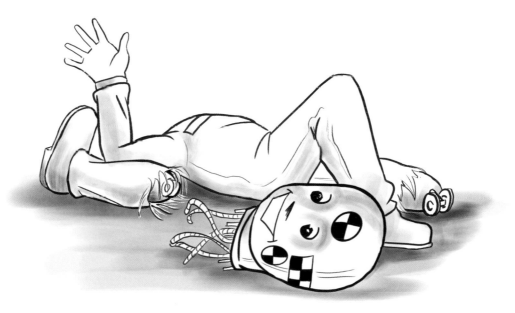

PEACHTREE

ATLANTA

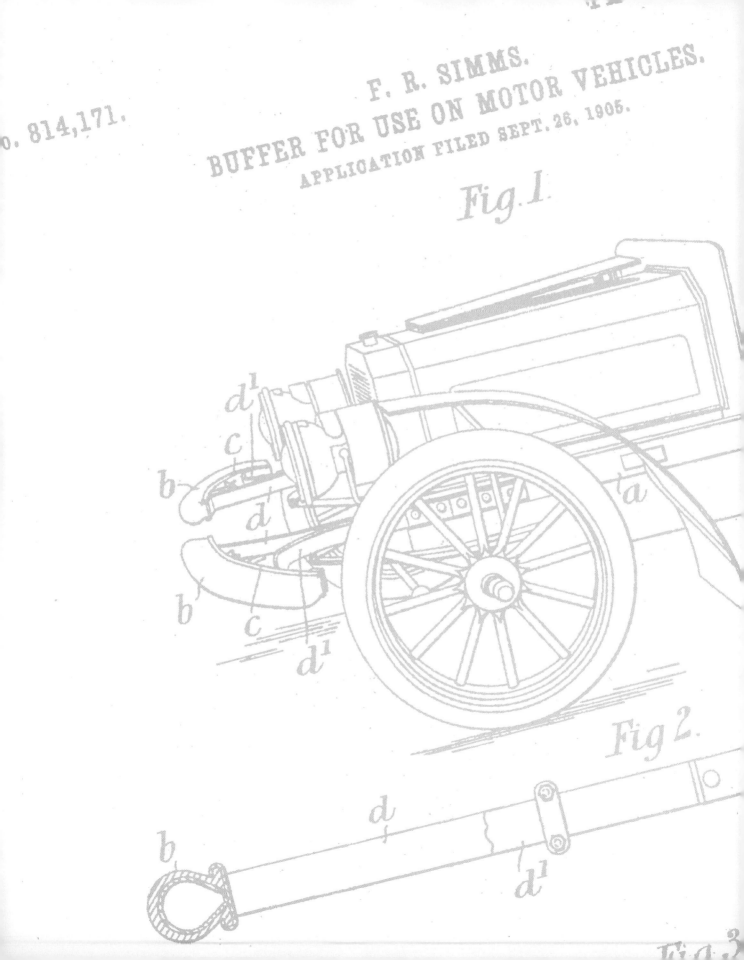

Fig.1.

Fig 2.

Fig.3

# Contents

# Time to Go

Time to go. You head to the car, ready for the 45-minute drive to school. As you open the car door, you brace yourself for the drive. Will your mom pepper you with questions about the day ahead? Or will you be captive to her radio choices yet again?

You climb into the front seat.

Wait. Your mom's not driving. In fact, the driver's seat is empty. You look around.

Where is the steering wheel? The brake? The gas pedal? You may not know how to drive yet, but you know those pieces belong in a car.

Then you see the two big buttons on the dashboard. They say Stop and Go.

Do you dare?

You look around again. Taking a deep breath, you push Go.

The engine starts.

The doors lock.

You hastily put on your seat belt.

The car backs slowly out of the driveway and heads down the road toward your school.

How cool.

Guess it's your day. You reach up and flip on the radio. Your favorite tunes dance along the airwaves. Ah…you are traveling in style.

*A Waymo
self-driving car*

Could you really have a driverless car take you to school? Maybe someday. Right now, none of the self-driving cars are set up to drive people to school. They are all still in their testing phase.

But a few have been spotted driving around towns. The Google self-driving car, now known as Waymo, has over three million miles (4.8 million kilometers) under its belt and has even been sighted safely navigating the Pacific Coast Highway—during high traffic times, no less. Autonomous cars are set to transform transportation as we know it.

Self-driving cars are said to be among the safest cars in the world. After all, they are "driven" by complex computer programming and robotics, rather than fallible humans. To ensure the utmost safety of the passengers, engineers have spent many years perfecting the design.

But the real stars of the self-driving cars are not human. None of these cars, nor the regular ones we drive today, would be possible without the selfless dedication and adventurous spirit of our friends, the crash-test dummies.

Let's take a look at how those intrepid travelers paved the way for safer travel—with the help of some humans, of course.

# chapter 1

# Under the Hood and Behind the Wheel

You probably don't think much about safety when you climb into a car. You buckle your seat belt, and then you just assume that the car is safe, right? It might surprise you to learn that it took many years, and thousands of crash tests, to create the safe vehicles you ride around in.

# Starting the Journey

Cars haven't always been as safe as they are today. In fact, the early cars were downright dangerous. They didn't even have bumpers, seat belts, or airbags.

Fortunately, engineers recognized the problems and set to work fixing them. But some of the solutions they came up with were a bit, well…puzzling. Here are just a few:

- a bumper that scooped up pedestrians in a big net so that the car didn't run over them
- a windshield that popped out in case of an accident, so the driver could slide out and across the hood
- a safety zone next to the steering wheel where the driver could dive during a crash
- a curved rearview mirror that gave a wider—but distorted—view

These sound like crazy options, and yet at one time, they were all used as safety devices. Today, the vehicles we drive are equipped with much more reliable means of protection. Before we start our journey, let's take a look at some essential facts about cars and care safety.

What are the important parts of a car? Turn the page and let's find out.

# What Makes a Car Go?

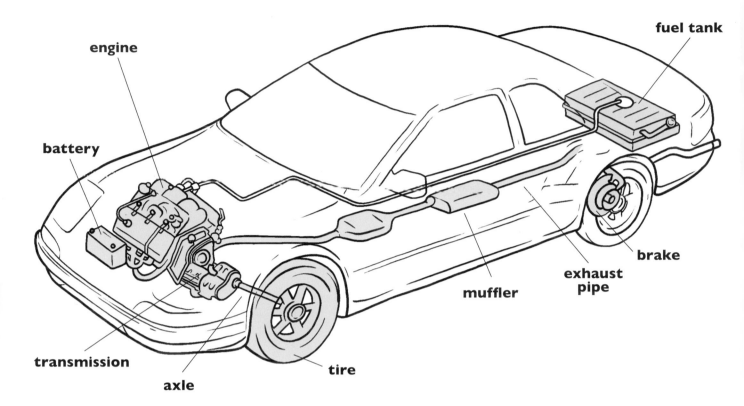

**These are some of the critical parts of a car:**

- **engine**: provides energy for the car to move
- **battery**: provides power to the engine
- **transmission**: allows the engine to shift to higher or lower gears for speed
- **axle**: holds two wheels together and supports the car
- **tires**: provide a solid surface on the road to allow the wheels to move smoothly
- **muffler**: keeps the sound of the motor from being so loud
- **exhaust pipe**: directs gas fumes away from the inside of the car
- **brake**: stops the car from moving
- **fuel tank**: stores the fuel needed to start and run the engine

# What Makes a Car Safe?

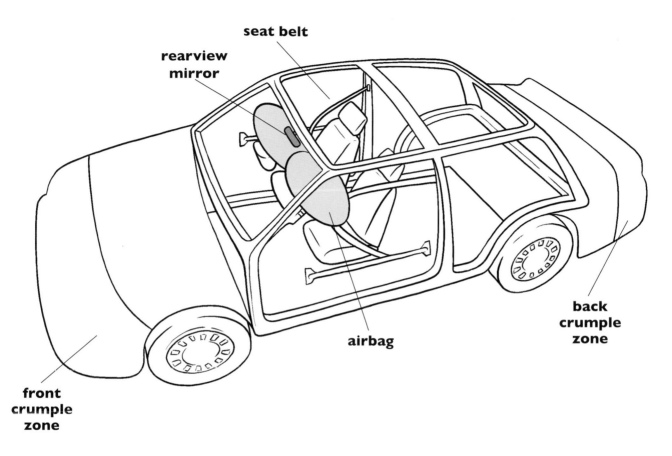

**These are some of the important safety features of a car:**

- **crumple zone:** structures located and front and back that are intended to crumple in order to absorb the force of an impact
- **seat belt:** straps that keep passengers in place and protect them from impact or dangerous movement
- **airbag:** device that inflates and deflates quickly to protect the driver
- **rearview mirror:** mirror located inside the vehicle to provide a view behind the car
- **side-view mirror:** mirror located on each front door, to provide views of each side

# What Does a Safety Designer Do?

*Designers at work in 1961*

An engineer is a person who designs and builds products such as car engines. There are all sorts of engineers. Some of them work with car companies to improve vehicle safety; they are called safety designers. Their jobs may include the following responsibilities:

- identifying the best and strongest materials
- creating the most energy-efficient structures
- considering the safety of the driver, the passengers, and even the family pet

Any good engineer needs data to produce a finished product, like a safe car. Engineers follow six basic guidelines when they are trying to develop a new product:

1. Ask questions and define the problem.
2. Imagine solutions by designing models.
3. Plan and carry out investigations.
4. Evaluate and interpret data using mathematical thinking.
5. Make improvements and modify design as necessary.
6. Build and test new prototypes.

Car safety engineers have to think about each of these steps when they create new cars. Thankfully, when they go to test their ideas, they have a little help.

# A Little Help

Yes, that's right. Safety engineers get information from crash-test dummies. These helpful figures are known as anthropomorphic test devices (ATDs). An ATD is designed to mimic a human's movement during a car accident.

The National Transportation Safety Board (NTSB) estimates that the equipment designed with the help of crash-test dummies has saved the lives of over 330,000 people since 1960.

Crash-test dummies have been subjected to many different kinds of crashes, including

- front impact
- side impact
- rear impact

After each test, the dummies are carefully inspected to see how they had been "injured." They have taken hits that have torn off limbs and caved in chests. They have been catapulted through windows and sunroofs and across the hoods of cars. From this data, engineers have been able to design solutions to make safer cars. Those solutions include

- improved seat belts
- softer windshields
- headrests to prevent whiplash

And these solutions saved lives.

As safety designers learned more, they modified the dummies to different shapes and sizes so they could continue making huge improvements to car safety for the future. Now there's a whole family.

*Two Hybrid II 50th percentile dummies*

In the 1980s and 1990s, the NHTSA featured two dummies in an ad campaign intended to get people to "buckle up to save lives." Following the campaign, seat belt usage by both drivers and passengers increased to almost 84%.

# Meet the Family

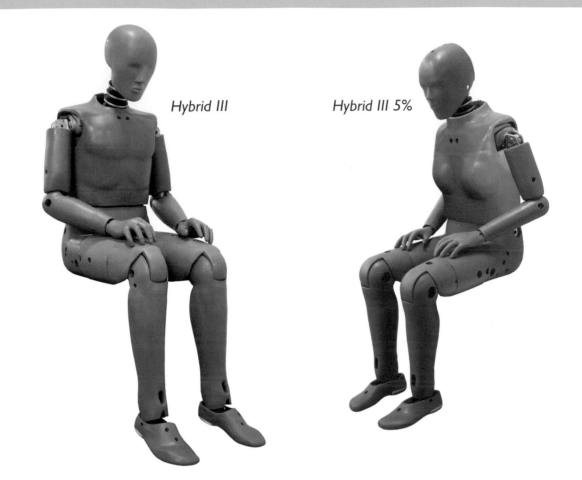

*Hybrid III*          *Hybrid III 5%*

*Crash-test dummy dog*

We crash-test dummies have been around since the 1950s, and we plan to be around for a whole lot longer. Let me introduce you to our family.

There's me, Hybrid III. I'm based on a male human who is 5 feet 9 inches tall (175 centimeters) and weighs 170 pounds (77 kilograms). Slim and trim, that's me.

My better half is Hybrid III 5%. She is based on a human female, approximately 5 feet tall (152 centimeters) and 108 pounds (49 kilograms).

My three "kids" are sized for children, ages ten, six, and three years.

Don't forget Fido! He's one of us. We want to keep our four-legged friends safe too.

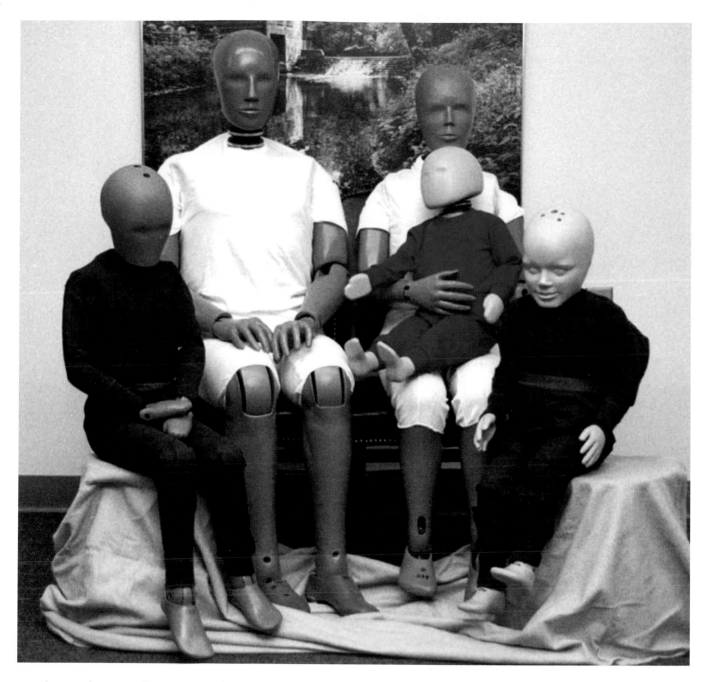

As we've aged, some adjustments have been made to our technology. Engineers have created new members of our family—specialized ones—for use in certain crash tests. You will meet them along the way.

For now, adjust your side mirrors and buckle up your seat belt. Let's get ready to cruise through some of the important aspects of car safety!

*Hybrid III 95% male, Hybrid III 5% female, and ten, six, and three-year-old child dummies*

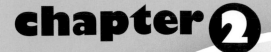

# chapter 2

# Bumper Cars

Bumpers. Who needs them? Humans do. Just ask Henry Bliss, the very first American killed in a car accident. In 1889, he stepped out of a streetcar and was immediately hit by a taxi; he died of his injuries the next day.

# What Does a Bumper Do?

*Front bumper on a Simms-Welbeck car*

A bumper is intended to protect the people inside a car during an accident. Before the bumper was invented, collisions were pretty messy. Tires got entangled, frames were mangled, and engines were set at odd angles.

Of course, none of this was great for the people inside or outside the car either. Sometimes they were just as jumbled up as the car itself, with the bumps and bruises to prove it.

The bumper helped to change all that. It provided a sort of barrier that kept colliding cars farther apart. That kept the driver and passengers safer.

In 1905, Frederick Simms patented the first bumper for his Simms-Welbeck car. Two simple curved metal shields, mounted on the front of the car, would spring back during a collision, pushing the automobiles apart. Unfortunately, Simms was not a great businessman and his company did not last three years.

**The very first car had neither a bumper nor an engine in the front. If two cars collided, the drivers' legs could become tangled, since the cars had no "bodies" to protect them.**

# Hanging Out in Front

*Cowcatcher test, Washington, DC, 1924*

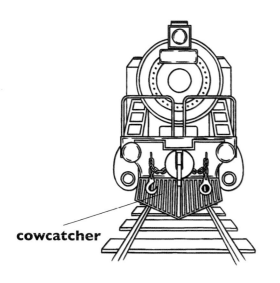

cowcatcher

The original cowcatcher was found on the front of a train. If a locomotive encountered a cow on the tracks, the cowcatcher would scoop it off and prevent a derailment.

Car engineers thought a cowcatcher might also work on a car. The first automobile version was shaped like a big net. It was attached to the front of the car, just above the ground. If the car hit a pedestrian, the bumper would knock him into the net, so he wouldn't be run over.

Did it work? Well, sort of. The bumper did keep the pedestrian from being run over. But being "scooped" wasn't much fun. Since the bumper was located just below knee level, it hit the pedestrian's shin. (*Ouch!*) The impact would knock him back into the net. If he landed sideways, he was good. But if he fell forward or backward, his head might smash against the car. (*Clunk!*)

# Rolling Along

*Cowcatcher test, Paris, 1924*

The roller safety device was another early bumper idea. This scary looking contraption was made of a few bars that extended from the front of the car, just above the ground. When a pedestrian was knocked to the ground in a collision, the roller safety device was intended to sweep her before it, thus making sure the car didn't run her over. But the bumps, bruises, and scrapes of being pushed along the ground were not fun either. *Ow!*

# Model T

1928 Model A Ford

The first bumper stickers were used in the 1920s to advertise products. Election-related stickers appeared in 1930, but the big push was in the 1952 election when "I Like Ike" stickers were plastered on bumpers across the country.

In the early 1920s, Ford's Model T rolled off the production line. It had its very own bumper in front of the car...and another one on the back. The bumpers were made of two thin bars of metal connected by another straight metal bar to the car frame.

These bumpers looked nice, but didn't do much. In most collisions, they got all banged up. Sometimes they caused two cars to get tangled together. These bumpers were mostly just for show; they made the car look pretty, but they didn't make the car any safer.

# Glitz and Glam

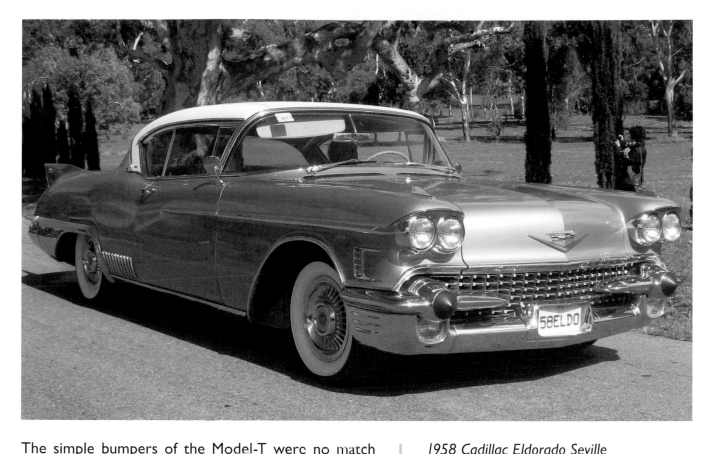

1958 Cadillac Eldorado Seville

The simple bumpers of the Model-T were no match for the glitz and glam of chrome. These shiny additions were found on cars manufactured from the 1940s through the 1960s. Compared to the bumpers of the 1920s, these were huge! They covered a large part of the front and back of the car.

Chrome bumpers provided more protection for the passengers during a collision. They were so heavy that they tended to absorb more damage than the car itself. But their weight made the car very heavy, which meant that it took a lot of gas to make the car go.

A fender is different from a bumper. A fender is installed over the wheel and blocks dirt and other debris thrown up from the road.

# Bumper Craze

During World War II, people replaced their metal bumpers with wooden ones. The metal was sent off to build tanks or ships. The wooden bumpers were ugly and flying shards after a collision were dangerous.

The Aurora, dubbed "the world's ugliest car," was designed in the 1950s by Alfred A. Juliano, a priest who was obsessed with car safety. The foam-filled bumper had its own shelf for scooping up pedestrians who got in the way. But the Aurora would have been quite expensive to produce, so only one prototype was ever made.

In the 1970s a new bumper "gushed" in. That is to say, engineers introduced a bumper filled with water. Why water? It's a very elastic fluid, meaning that it bounces back when hit. Think about a water balloon. Sometimes when you throw one, it doesn't break upon impact, but simply bounces off the object it hits. The water-filled bumper was intended to protect passengers by softening the impact of a collision. Of course, when the bumper collided with another car—*whoosh!*—water sprayed everywhere!

One brave volunteer even put his head between two water-filled bumpers. He got a little wet, but thankfully he was otherwise unhurt by the collision!

Engineers needed to understand how the human body is affected by a car accident. Before the development of ATDs, their options were limited.

Some engineers used cadavers to obtain car crash data. It's not as strange as it sounds. Human cadavers have been used in science for hundreds of years. Safety engineers have also used live animals, such as chimpanzees, hogs, or bears.

While it might seem a little gruesome, cadavers provide invaluable information to car manufacturers. Cadaver movement at the point of impact and beyond is filmed so engineers can see where the human body moves during an accident. Using X-rays and MRI scans, engineers can see what type of injuries a human might receive during a crash.

During an experiment, a cadaver is treated with the utmost respect. Relatives are informed and have consented to the tests. Safety engineers study every part of the body. When the research is complete, a cadaver is given a proper and respectful burial.

Don't have a cadaver? No problem. Use live humans! In the 1940s, safety engineers turned to the United States Air Force for help. Around that time, the Air Force was testing ejection seats. Following an impact, an ejection seat detaches from the airplane and is launched into the sky. This allows the pilot to deploy his parachute and avoid going down in a plane crash.

Ejection-seat testing was intended to explore the effect of abrupt deceleration on the human body. To do so, the Air Force used real people. A test subject was seated in a chair that was attached to a sled on a track. The sled was catapulted down the track toward a brick or concrete wall at extremely high speeds. The subjects also agreed to be bashed in the chest with heavy objects and sprayed with broken glass, all in the name of science.

*An ejection seat in action*

Colonel John Stapp of the Air Force was the first human crash-test dummy. He traveled at 632 mph (1017 kph) on a rocket sled with an open cockpit to see how the acceleration and forces affected humans. And he survived!

These tests, while very painful for the subjects and also dangerous, were critical for the development of the safety features of planes and cars.

*Lt. Col. John Stapp rides a rocket sled at Edwards Air Force Base*

# Sierra Sam Saves the Day

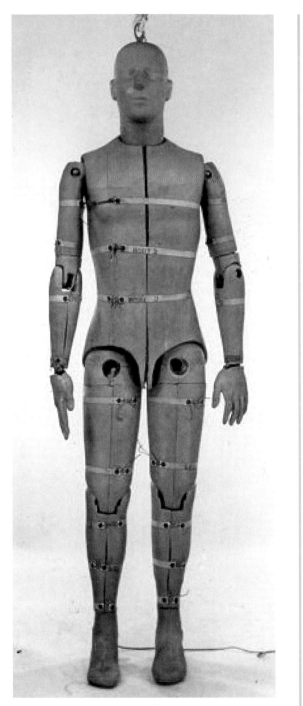

*Sierra Sam ATD used to test ejection seats*

In 1949, a nonhuman, but very humanlike dummy—an anthropomorphic test device (ATD)—was created. He was called Sierra Sam, in honor of the Sierra Engineering Company that designed him.

Sam's first mission was to test aircraft ejection seats for the Air Force. He was shot into the air many times (*Pfft!*) and he always landed with a bang—sometimes on his head. The data from these experiments inspired engineers at car companies. Maybe they, too, should use Sam as well. After all, the call for increasing the safety of cars was becoming really loud. People wanted safer cars.

But car-crash testing was not the same as ejection-seat testing. Sierra Sam needed a more fully formed body to provide the data needed. In 1968, the Sierra Engineering Company designed a new ATD to meet the car companies' needs. This version had a spine like a human's, but it was made out of metal. The neck had springs that could mimic the muscle movement of a human neck. It had joints, such as knees, elbows, and shoulders, in order for engineers to see how a human would move during an accident.

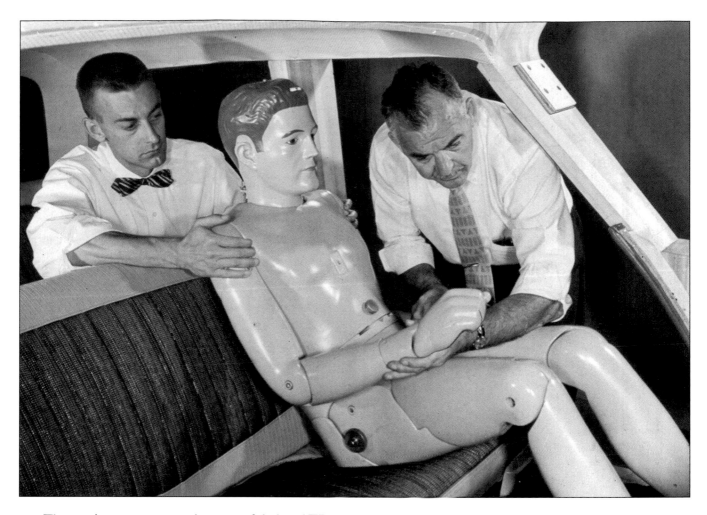

*Ford engineers adjust a crash-test dummy in 1960*

The real question was how useful this ATD would be to carmakers. For twenty years, safety tests had been done without a lot of guidelines. Engineers tested certain parts of the car, but not others. They used the data to improve some features, but never really looked at overall safety.

That all changed in 1971, when the National Highway Safety Transportation Administration (NHSTA) decided it was time for a stronger push to make cars safer. They wanted to significantly decrease the number of injuries or deaths from car accidents.

# Hybrid-III and Head-on Crashes

As technology improved, so did the crash-test dummies. Hybrid III was constructed in 1978, and has been used for the last thirty years.

The Hybrid III dummy is about the size of the average adult male. But there's not much else that is average about this dummy. Its upper body is composed of six high-strength steel ribs that compress just like your chest would upon impact with an object. If the impact would break your ribs, it will break Hybrid III's. Its lower body has a spine that curves just like yours does when you sit down. Its head and neck turn and bend just like yours do.

But most importantly, Hybrid III is full of electronics. Inside its body, it has accelerometers, potentiometers, and load cells, all of which tell engineers about the acceleration, deflection, and forces that each part of its body is feeling. This information is then used to make cars safer.

Hybrid III's job is to survive a frontal impact crash. This is what happens when an object strikes the front bumper of the car or when the car crashes into an object. The object can be another car, a tree, a guardrail, or even a person.

A Hybrid III may experience hundreds of crashes in its lifetime. It may endure hard hits to the head and chest, crunching of the legs and arms, and stretching of the neck. Head-on crashes into concrete barriers, sideswipes with a deformable sled "bumper," rear-end crashes that tear off bumpers—each of these provide helpful information.

But a crash-test dummy is useful only as long as it stays intact. For example, if its head flies off, then the dummy must be retired. A crash-test dummy without a head can't provide good data.

Recycling really is for everyone!

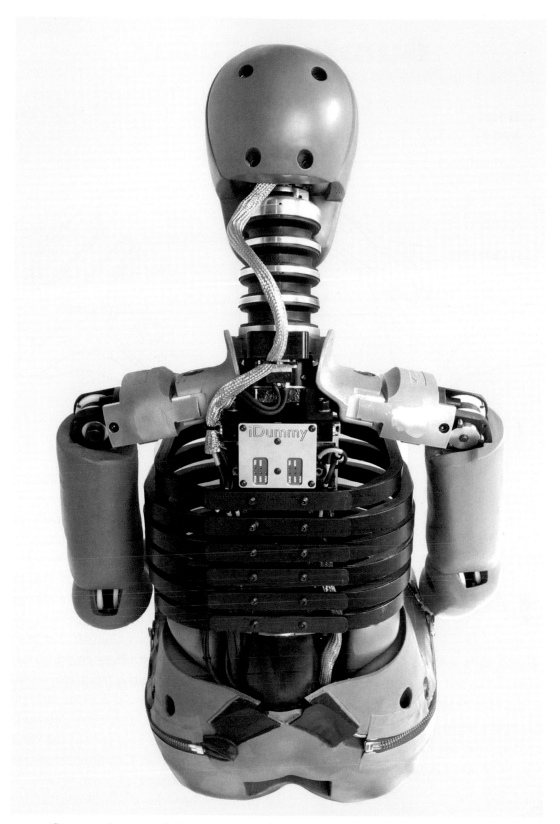

*iDummy data acquisition system and instrumentation cabling within an ATD*

# Bumpers Today

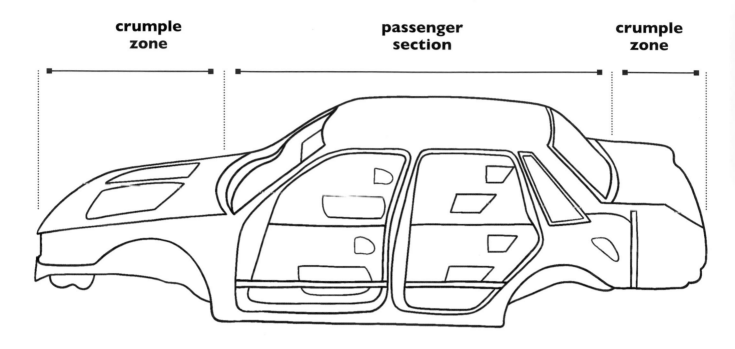

crumple zone

passenger section

crumple zone

**Bumpers were optional until 1971, when the NHTSA required them to be installed on all cars.**

What did engineers do with the information they'd gathered over many years of crash-test dummy data collection? They came up with a new plan for car construction. It was a pretty revolutionary idea: cars would no longer have bumpers.

Bumpers had been designed to absorb the force from an impact and reflect it back at the other car in the same way that the strings on a tennis racket bow in and bounce back as it hits the ball. But bumpers didn't always keep people safe. They could be torn off in an accident or pushed into the front seat, either of which could cause great harm to the driver and passengers.

Instead of bumpers, engineers designed something called a crumple zone. This part of the car is supposed to cave in when it is hit. Crumple zones are located at the front and back part of a car, where the bumpers used to be. When the front of the car is struck, the hood is pushed in, or crumpled.

*2018 Toyota Camry XLE*

Imagine an accordion. When you push on the ends, it slowly folds in. The same thing happens to the front of a car in a front-impact accident. The slow crumple allows some of the force from the impact to be absorbed into the car. This redirects the force away from the people inside.

Inside a car, the passengers are encased within a metal frame that keeps them safer. Think of it as a kind of cage. The frame surrounds the space from in front of the dashboard to behind the rear seats. Everything inside it is protected by the frame; it will not crumple when hit. Of course, that does not mean that people won't be injured in a crash, but crumple zones do help. They are found in almost every car on the market today.

Are today's bumpers safer than ever? Actually, no. They're largely cosmetic. Bumpers are almost invisible. Look at the car above. Can you tell that it has bumpers? Not really. The bumpers are now part of the frame. They are just there to help with catastrophic accidents and to make the car look good.

The credit for increased car safety goes to the engineers who created the new frame and protective zones on the car—and the crash-test dummies who helped. Don't forget them!

# Belt Me In!

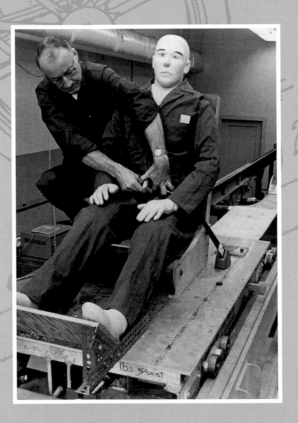

What is the first thing you do when you get into a car? You put on your seat belt! You probably don't even think about it. After all, it's the law. But it hasn't always been this way. In fact, seat belts weren't even standard features in cars until 1963, and the first state laws regulating their use wouldn't appear until 1984, almost one hundred years after the first car was developed.

# What Does a Seat Belt Do?

A seat belt is supposed to keep passengers safe during an accident—it should prevent them from slamming into the dashboard or the back of the front seat or sliding into each other. And most importantly, seat belts are designed to keep passengers from being thrown from the car. According to the Centers for Disease Control and Prevention (CDC), "seat belt use is the most effective way to save lives and reduce injuries in crashes."

The first cars didn't travel very fast, so manufacturers didn't see a need for seat belts. But doctors disagreed. They were first-hand witnesses to the terrible results of car crash ejections.

In the 1930s, a group of doctors got together and urged car companies to install some type of restraint system. A few of them even created their own version and started using the restraints in their own cars. They really didn't need to make their own. Seat belts had actually been invented back in 1885. Well, sort of.

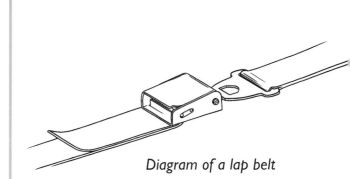

*Diagram of a lap belt*

In 2016, 23,714 people died in car crashes. More than half of teens and adults aged 20–44 who died were not buckled up.

33

# The Birth of Seat Belts

*George Cayley, inventor of the first seat belt*

*Diagram from Edward Claghorn's patent for "devices for lowering persons from buildings or the like by making use of rope-lowering devices with brakes sliding on the rope"*

The first seat belt was invented in the nineteenth century by George Cayley, for use in gliders.

In 1885, Edward Claghorn patented a belt that was to be used for "securing the person to a fixed object." Interestingly enough he did not mention cars in his application. This belt could be used for anything—boats, planes, cars, or even roller coaster seats.

The earliest versions of automotive seat belts were lap belts, also called two-point belts. They secured the passenger at two points—one on either side of the body. Race car drivers were the first people to use lap belts regularly. They understood the importance of staying in the car during an accident.

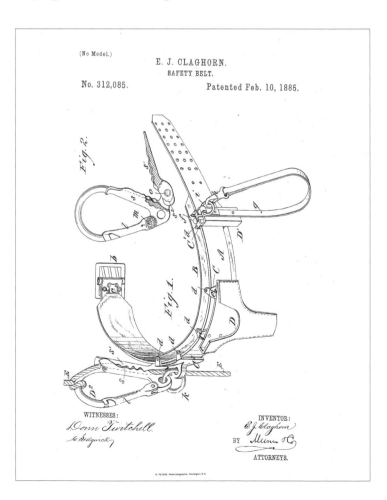

# Lap Belts—Safe or Sorry?

In 1956, Chrysler, Ford, and Volvo offered lap belts as optional equipment. This meant that the buyer would have to pay extra to purchase them. At the time, few customers were willing to spend the money. You could say that safety took a "back seat" to cost at this point. Over the next few years, people began see the benefits of wearing a seat belt.

But lap belts could also be dangerous. They were good at keeping a person inside the car, for sure. The problem was that they sometimes caused horrible internal injuries. When a person is in a car accident, the impact slams her forward at a high force—but the belt pulls her back. This can put enormous pressure on the lower body, possibly injuring the intestines, stomach, liver, and other organs. Not good.

In fact, in 1958, a New Hampshire–based motor vehicle research organization announced that the "seat belt can be dangerous to the average user under most crash conditions." They said that the seat belt "was a tool of commercialism used at the expense of human life and injuries."

Despite the safety concerns, the use of lap belts increased. By 1963, more than twenty states had laws that required the use of lap belts in the front seat. That changed things completely. Now car companies started to install them in every car. By 1967, lap belts were being placed in the back seats of cars as well. In 1996, the Society of Automotive Engineers estimated that the continuous use of seat belts had reduced deaths from car accidents by as much as 50 percent and serious injuries by more than 60 percent.

Look, Ma! No hands!

# The Physics of a Car Crash

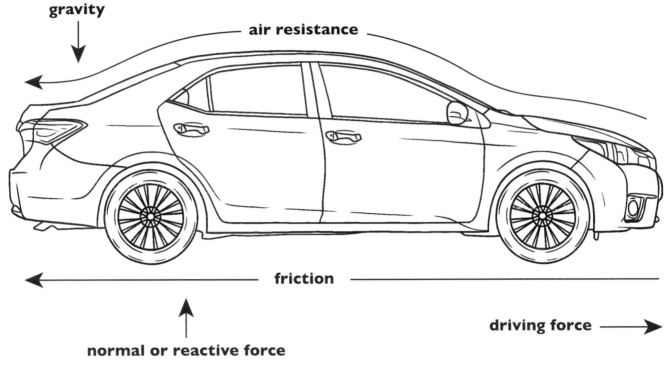

gravity

air resistance

friction

driving force

normal or reactive force

## What forces act upon a car while it is moving?

These forces act upon it to slow it down.

- **Gravity** pushes down on the car.
- **Normal (or reactive) force** pushes up from the road onto the car. It is the opposite of gravity.
- **Friction** is created by from the tires rolling on the road.
- **Air resistance** is caused by the air flowing over the outside of the car.

Only one force works to move a car forward.

- **Driving (or forward) force** is provided by the engine pushing the car forward.

In order for a car to move, the driving force must be strong enough to overcome all of the other forces, which are slowing it down.

## What forces act on the body during a collision?

There are three laws of motion known as Newton's Laws, after Sir Isaac Newton, an English mathematician and physicist who defined them in his 1687 book *Philosophiæ Naturalis Principia*.

- **First law:** An object in motion will tend to stay in motion unless acted upon. A car traveling at 30 mph (48 kph) will continue to move at that rate unless the driver steps on the brake to slow it down.
- **Second law:** The heavier an object is, the more force it takes to increase its speed. A car is heavy, so it requires a lot of force (from the engine) to get it to move. And the more force the driver applies, the faster the car will travel. If the driver pushes down hard on the gas pedal, the car will go faster.
- **Third law:** For every action, there is an equal and opposite reaction. If a car slams into a tree, the car will be pushing on the tree, but the tree will also be pushing back on the car. That's what causes the hood and bumper to crumple.

## How exactly does a person get injured?

When a car is in motion, the passengers inside are traveling at the same speed as the car. If the car is traveling at 30 mph (48 kph), so are the people.

A moving car follows Newton's first law of motion, which means that it will keep moving unless something stops it. When a moving car hits an obstacle—another car or perhaps a tree—it will stop immediately upon impact.

But the passengers inside keep moving. The seat belt is the only thing that keeps them in place in the car. If they are not restrained, they could be thrown out of the car.

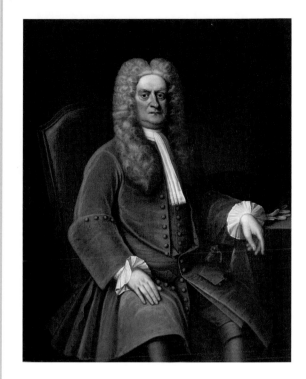

*portrait of Sir Isaac Newton*

# Crazy Safety Ideas

Seat belts were intended to help people survive car accidents. People had some other crazy ideas too.

For a short time, car designers thought that the passengers of the car would be safer if they were ejected onto the hood during an accident, so they designed a windshield that popped out when the car was struck. One car that incorporated this design was the Tucker 48, also known as the Tucker Torpedo, designed by Chicago policeman Preston Tucker in 1948. In addition to pop-out windshield glass, the Torpedo also included impact-absorbing bumpers and a third headlight that turned with the front wheels to shine more light on the road. Under the front dashboard was a safety chamber. Just before impact, passengers "could dive to safety."

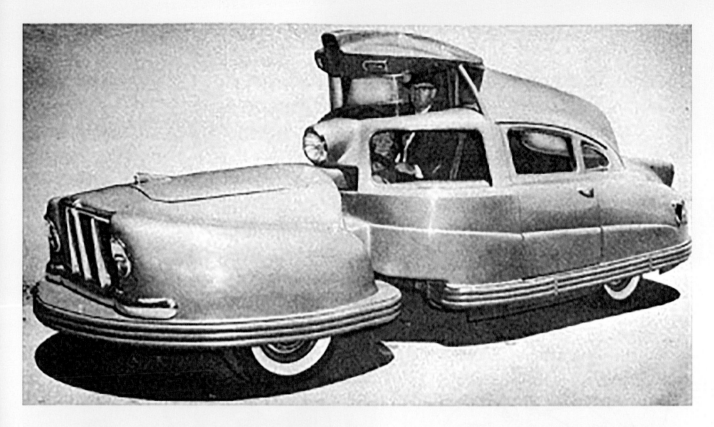

The Cornell-Liberty Safety Car, created in 1957, had some good safety features, including front-seat headrests, wrap-around bumpers, and three-point seat belts. The enclosed driver's seat—located in the middle of the front seat—made the car look a bit like a spaceship. The front passenger seats faced the rear of the car. And did you see the steering wheel? It looks like the handlebars of a bicycle. Crazy!

Or you could buy the Sir Vival car! You'd be sure to survive any crash—assuming you could pay the high price and you didn't feel embarrassed driving this monstrosity down the road. Created in 1958, the Sir Vival sported all the latest in safety inventions: air-filled rubber bumpers, pivoting doors that stayed closed during an accident, and best of all, a two-section body that broke apart during a collision. The steering wheel was located in the center of the car. No working models of this car were ever built. The designer couldn't come up with the ten thousand dollars needed to build one.

# Three Is Better Than Two

*Nils Bohlin, inventor of the three-point seat belt*

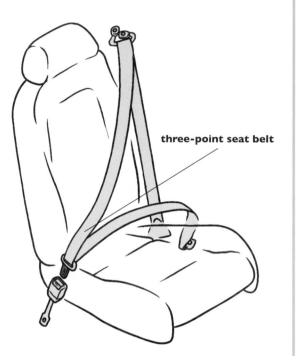

three-point seat belt

**What happened to lap belts? They are still used today, but not in cars. You will find them the next time you fly the friendly skies.**

If two points on a belt were dangerous, then why not just add a third? That's exactly what Swedish inventor Nils Bohlin did. The three-point seat belt he designed secured a passenger across both the lap and the shoulder. This tiny change was enough to keep a person in her seat during a accident.

In 1959, the first three-point belt was installed in a Volvo as an optional addition. Volvo also offered the newly designed belt to other car manufacturers at no added cost. By 1968, the three-point seat belt was required to be standard equipment in all European and US cars. At the time of Bohlin's death in 2002, Volvo estimates that his three-point seat belt invention had saved over 1 million lives.

# Automatic Seat Belts

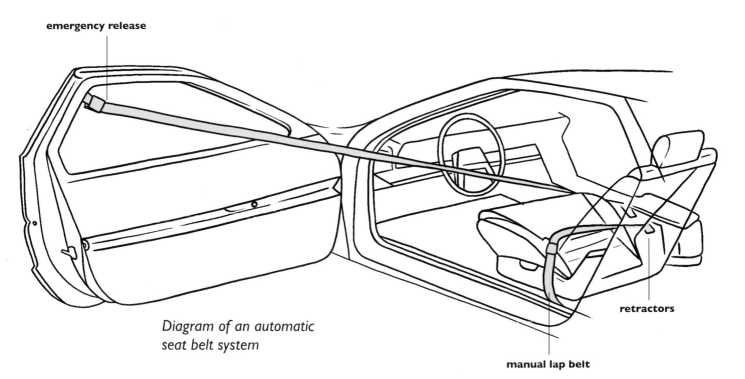

emergency release

retractors

manual lap belt

*Diagram of an automatic
seat belt system*

For a short time, companies tried automatic seat belts.
When the driver shut the car door, the belt slid into
position, following a track along the door.

These belts didn't work very well. Sometimes they
were too tight or too loose. They were awkward and
people often became tangled up in them when getting
in or out.

Automatic seat belts could also be dangerous. If the
door flew open during an accident, the seat belt went
with it, leaving the passenger at risk of flying out of the
car.

# Is Four the Magic Number?

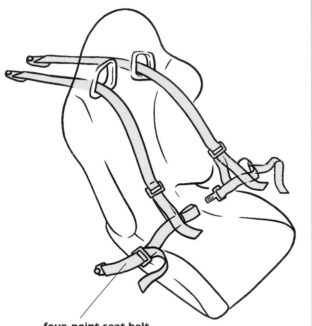

**four-point seat belt**

Are four-point seat belts the wave of the future? Perhaps. They already exist in race cars and planes. You will also find them children's car seats.

A four-point seat belt is attached at four points: over each shoulder and alongside each hip. It is the safest option for cars that have a tendency to roll over, such as a sports utility vehicle (SUV).

But this type of belt is not always comfortable and it is sometimes hard to get into. Engineers are still debating the design of the four-point belt. Crash-test dummy studies have shown that the rib cage is the best part of the body to absorb the force of impact. So some engineers argue that the four-point harness should cross over the ribcage, like an X across the body.

That design would be really tough to fit to people of different sizes. And if it's uncomfortable, most people won't wear it. So, for now, the four-point harness will remain on the drawing board and not in a car.

The first car seat for infants was basically a sack. The baby was placed inside the sack which was attached to the backseat with a drawstring.

# Seat Belts Today

Today, the three-point seat belt is still the most widely used restraint system. But changes have been made.

The center of gravity of an SUV is higher than that of a sedan. That makes it top heavy and therefore more likely to tip over than a sedan. You may have heard the term "rollover" used to describe an accident. That word came into use after so many SUVs rolled over during collisions.

When a car rolls over, a three-point seat belt doesn't always stay in the proper position. If the shoulder strap doesn't fit tightly, then the person might slide out.

After crash-test dummy testing, engineers came up with a solution. They added something to the belt called a pretensioner— a sensor that detects an abrupt decrease in motion. The pretensioner automatically reels in the seat belt, making it tight across the body. This keeps you firmly in your seat—and in the car. Pretensioners are especially important in the event of a rollover. If your seat belt is loose, you are more apt to fall out of the car if you are upside-down.

After all the testing, the engineering, and the sacrifice of the crash-test dummies, what is the biggest problem with seat belts today? Getting people to wear them. Even though police encourage people to wear them—and charge them fines if they don't—some people still don't buckle up. They say seat belts are uncomfortable, that it takes too long to put them on, that they're only going a few miles down the road…

Whatever excuse you come up with, just know that there isn't a good one. It is a proven fact: seat belts save lives!

# Hit the Brakes!

As long as there have been moving vehicles there have been brakes. Bicycles, trains, and airplanes all have brakes—even horse-drawn carriages had them. Why? It has to do with Newton's First Law of Motion. Remember? An object in motion will stay in motion unless acted upon by an outside force. In the case of a car in motion, the force is a brake.

# What Do Brakes Do?

Brakes use friction to slow down the wheels of a car. Friction is a force that holds back a moving object.

The very first brakes were made of simple wooden blocks. The blocks were placed next to the rim of the wheel, but not touching it. If the driver wanted to slow down or stop, she pulled a long lever attached to the brake, which pushed the block against the wheel. The friction between the block and the rim caused the motion to decrease.

For the next two thousand years, the brake structure stayed the same, but people found better materials. In the American west, people used cast iron instead of wood in the construction of locomotive brakes; they needed a something stronger to stop a large, heavy vehicle faster and more efficiently. It worked, to an extent, but there were still runaway trains that couldn't be stopped by the block-and-lever method.

There is another relationship between friction and cars. When a wheel rolls across a surface, like a road, it experiences friction. As the wheel rubs against the road, it slows down. The amount of friction produced depends upon the type of surface. A rough surface like a rocky road will generate more friction than a smooth road made of blacktop or asphalt. Improved roads made driving much easier.

Give it a try! Take any type of ball and roll it across a table or other flat surface. It goes pretty fast, doesn't it? Now take that same ball outside and roll it across a level sidewalk or a gravel driveway. Does the ball appear to roll more slowly than it did on a smooth surface? It should. Friction from the rough sidewalk or gravel surface will slow it down.

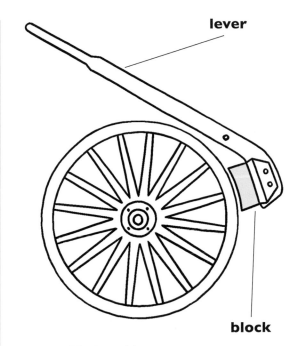

**lever**

**block**

*Basic block-and-lever braking system*

**Wooden blocks were used as brakes on two-wheeled vehicles during the Roman Empire.**

45

# Drum Brakes

*Louis Renault, inventor of the drum brake system*

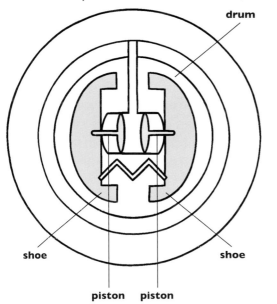

*The interior of a drum brake system*

In the early 1900s, the car gradually replaced the horse and carriage, and soon it was time for brakes to change as well. Cars had rubber tires and the block-and-lever system just wasn't enough to stop them.

In 1902, Louis Renault developed the drum brake. The drum was a metal cylinder that spun with the car movement. Inside the drum were two pads, called "shoes." When the driver applied the brakes, the shoes were pushed against the drum, which slowed its spinning. As the drum slowed, it applied pressure to the wheel, which made it slow and then stop.

Think of it this way. What if you're riding your bicycle and you want to stop but you don't want use your brake? What do you do? You put your feet out and drag them along the ground. The friction from your feet slows down the turning of the wheels and your bike stops. A drum brake also works by using friction.

The first drum brake was a manual system. It required the driver to pull a lever to apply force to the brake. At first, the drum brakes were located on the outside of the wheel. But they were exposed to dust, water, and heat, which made them break down, so they were moved inside the wheel.

# Fluids Are Better Than Drums

Drum brakes were hard to use when a car was traveling at a speeds higher than 10 to 15 mph (16 to 24 kph). In 1918, Malcolm Loughead introduced a much easier way to stop a car. He created hydraulic brakes—brakes that contained fluid.

Imagine a water balloon. If you squeeze one side, all of the water rushes to the other side of the balloon. The pressure that results pushes that side of the balloon out.

Hydraulic brakes are based on the same concept. If you push on one end of a container filled with liquid, the fluid is forced to the other end. Loughead realized that if you could capture the pressure that results, you could use it to stop a car.

How does a fluid-filled brake work?
1. The driver steps on the brake pedal.
2. The pressure from the pedal pushes oil into a hose.
3. The oil travels through the hose and fills two pistons.
4. The pistons push the shoes into the wheel.
5. The wheel slows down.

Hydraulic brakes allow a driver to slow a car down quickly and evenly, which may prevent an accident.

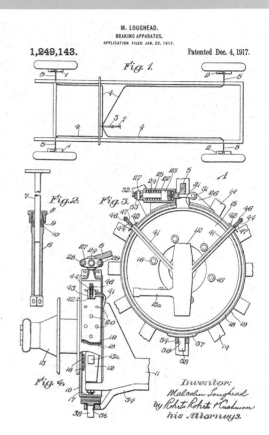

Diagram from Malcolm Loughead's patent for hydraulic brakes

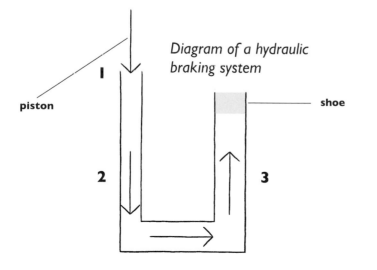

Diagram of a hydraulic braking system

piston

shoe

**The first set of hydraulic brakes was installed in a Duesenberg Model A car in 1929.**

# Disc Brakes

Drum brakes have some problems. The shoes (brake pads) create friction within the drum; too much friction can overheat the pads, causing the brakes to fail. It could be dangerous if a driver's brakes failed when she was trying to slow her vehicle on a steep hill.

So engineers tried something new. They attached a disc to the outside of the wheel. This way, the disc slowed the wheel but created less friction than a brake pad.

How does a disc braking system work?

1. The driver steps on the brake pedal.
2. The brake pedal pushes a piston into the fluid, compressing it.
3. The compressed fluid pushes down on the other, wider piston
4. The wider piston pinches the two brake pads together against the drum.
5. The disc and then the wheel slow down.

Each wheel has its own brake system. When one pedal is pushed, all four wheels experience all of these steps at the same time.

*Diagram of a disc brake system*

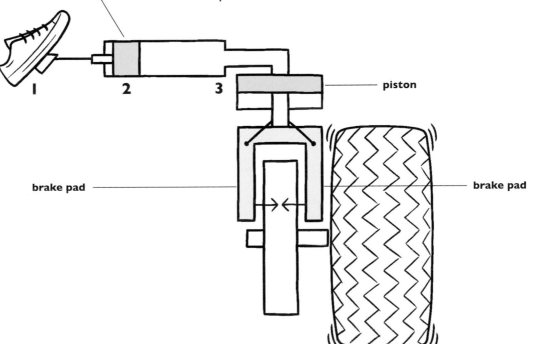

piston

piston

1    2    3

brake pad

brake pad

# Hitting the Skids

Disc brakes worked well in certain situations, but they still weren't effective enough on wet or icy pavement. If a driver pressed down too hard on the brakes, the car could skid.

What causes a car to skid? If the driver puts too much pressure on the brakes, this slams the discs into the wheels, which causes the wheels to lock, or stop turning abruptly. Just because the wheels have stopped turning doesn't mean the car has stopped moving, especially on a wet or icy surface. It still takes some time for the car to stop after the brakes are applied. The time and distance the car continues moving after braking depends on how fast it is going and how hard the driver has applied the brake.

A driver can't steer very well in a skid. That means the car's direction is unpredictable.

Skids became things of the past with the creation of antilock braking system (ABS). As their name suggests, antilock brakes don't lock up. And if the brakes don't lock, then it's possible to steer while skidding. With ABS it is no longer necessary for a driver to pump the brakes to try to prevent a skid. Instead, the system pulses or pushes each individual brake line in short bursts.

ABS is always paired with electronic brake force distribution (EBD). EBD varies the force each individual brake is applying at one time. This keeps the wheels from stopping too quickly and locking up.

**The first antilock brakes were so loud, they actually scared drivers and made the situation worse.**

Look out!

49

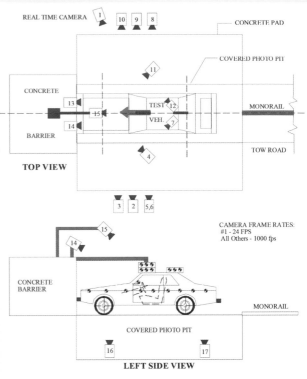

High-speed cameras are located all over the test area so they can capture the crash test from many angles.

Engineers start out with a new car in perfect condition.

Crash-test dummies are placed in the seats and buckled in.

Engineers put stickers and sensors on all sides and parts of the vehicle. This will allow them to calculate speed and direction when they examine video and photos after the test. On the left, you can see the wall this car is going to hit.

Vrooom.... Bam! Crunch! Oof!

Now that the test is done, engineers will study all the data that was collected. They will inspect the dummies to see if and how they were "injured."

# chapter 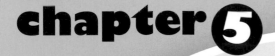 5

# Airbag Away

*Bam!* Your car slams into an obstacle. The impact sends your body flying forward. Thankfully, your seat belt locks and yanks your torso into your seat. But unfortunately, your head keeps moving, dangerously close to the steering wheel. And then *Bam! Whoosh!* Another impact. But this one's inside your car.

# What Does an Airbag Do?

When an airbag inflates, it provides a barrier that protects passengers inside a car during an accident. It is literally a bag full of gas that redistributes the force of an impact over a greater area. Airbags are located in the steering wheel, dashboard, and side doors of most vehicles made today.

In 1998, federal legislation required that airbags be installed in all new cars. Today they are found in just about every car on the road.

*Without an airbag, the driver's head hits a small part of the steering wheel.*

**When the Mars Rover descended to the planet's surface, it was encased in 4 huge airbags that prevented it from being damaged when it landed.**

*An airbag redistribtes the force of impact across the driver's body.*

# The First Airbags

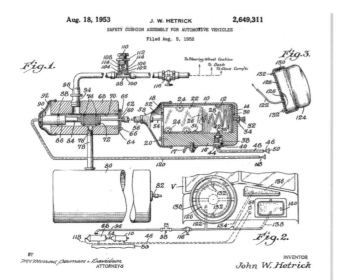

Aug. 18, 1953    J. W. HETRICK    2,649,311
SAFETY CUSHION ASSEMBLY FOR AUTOMOTIVE VEHICLES
Filed Aug. 5, 1952

BY
*Mc Morrow, Berman + Davidson*
ATTORNEYS

INVENTOR
*John W. Hetrick*

*Diagram from John W. Hetrick's patent for a "safety cushion assembly for automotive vehicles"*

John W. Hetrick designed the first airbag, after he and his family were in a car accident. Hetrick, his wife, and their daughter were traveling when he swerved to avoid a large rock in the road. The car skidded into a ditch. Everyone was fine, but later he remembered that both he and his wife threw their arms out to keep their daughter from hitting the dashboard.

Like a good engineer, Hetrick was inspired by the experience. What if he could create some kind of inflatable device that would come out of the car dashboard or steering wheel to do the same thing their arms had done? So he got to work, and in 1953, he received a patent for his airbag design.

Hetrick was an industrial engineer with the United States Navy. He based his design on an inflatable canvas cover that fits over a torpedo. His airbag featured three parts: an air accumulator, an inflatable cushion, and a release valve.

The concept was pretty advanced for the time, which meant that the technology to support it hadn't been created yet. None of the sensors developed at the time could react quickly enough to help people during an accident. The cushion material available was rough and hard to inflate. As a result, during the first tests, the airbags caused as many injuries as the crashes.

In 1968, mechanical engineer Allan K. Breed created the first electromechanical airbag sensor for cars. Breed got the idea from safety sensors that were developed for the United States military. These new sensors were capable of detecting, evaluating, and deploying an airbag quickly and efficiently.

Breed's sensors did so well that he kept working on car safety. Over the years, his company, Key Safety Systems, created more than a dozen new and improved safety features for cars, including developing vents so that the airbag can deflate faster.

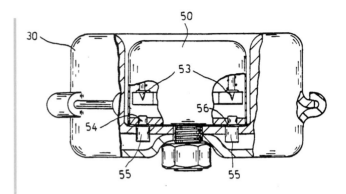

*Diagram from Allan K. Breed's patent for a "method and apparatus for gas generator initiation from external sensor"*

Oof! That's going to leave a mark!

55

# Timing Is Everything

**airbag**

*Airbag prior to inflation*

A standard airbag takes between 0.01 and 0.03 seconds to fully inflate. Humans blink their eyes every 0.1 to 0.4 seconds.

Timing is the most important aspect of an airbag. In order to provide the most protection, it must inflate immediately after an accident.

Why so fast? The impact, the movement of passengers' bodies, and even the deployment of the airbag happen in less than three seconds.

Inflating the bag with air, like a balloon, would take too long. How long does it take to pump up a bike tire? At least a few minutes.

An airbag doesn't have that much time. It has less than 0.3 seconds to prevent a passenger's head from hitting the steering wheel, dashboard, or window.

A chemical reaction is the only way to inflate an airbag that quickly. The "air" that fills up the bag is actually a nitrogen gas created by three quick-acting chemical reactions.

An uninflated airbag contains a pellet composed of three gases:

- sodium azide ($NaN_3$)
- potassium nitrate ($KNO_3$)
- silicon dioxide ($SiO_2$)

Upon impact, the sodium azide ignites, reaching 572 degrees Fahrenheit (300 degrees Celsius).

The heat causes the sodium azide to break down into two different molecules:

- sodium (Na)
- nitrogen gas ($N_2$)

The nitrogen gas fills the airbag, expanding at the rate of 150 to 250 mph (241 to 402 kph). The rapid expansion causes the airbag to burst through its cover and create a massive cushion for the passenger. What happens to the sodium? This highly flammable element can cause an explosion on its own. That's why the pellet also contains potassium nitrate and silicon dioxide—to counteract the sodium.

The second reaction is between the potassium nitrate and the sodium. This produces

- potassium oxide ($K_2O$)
- sodium oxide ($Na_2O$)
- more nitrogen gas ($N_2$)

The final reaction occurs when the silicon dioxide reacts with the potassium and sodium dioxides from the second reaction to produce alkaline silicate, or glass.

This reaction neutralizes the sodium. That's a good thing, because if the sodium got out, it would react with the water in the air to produce sodium hydroxide (NaOH). Sodium hydroxide is very toxic and could burn passengers' noses, eyes, and skin. Instead it is turned into alkaline silicate, harmless glass particles.

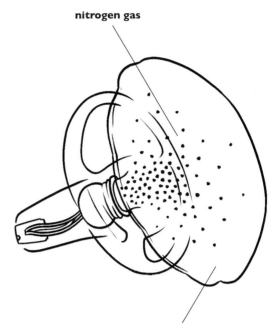

*Airbag filled with nitrogen gas following a collision*

The idea behind the chemical reaction that inflates an airbag is actually similar to the way a solid rocket booster works. But of course, on a much smaller scale.

# What Inflates Must Deflate

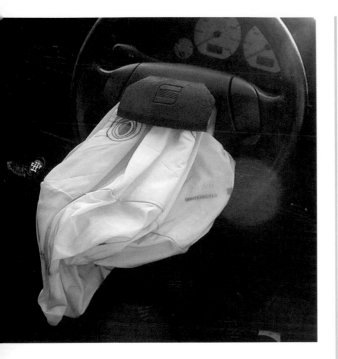

*A deflated airbag*

It only takes about 40 milliseconds for an airbag to inflate following impact—and then it must deflate just as fast. Why?

The force of inflation averages about 200 mph (322 kph). That's faster than a professional ballplayer can throw a baseball. You really don't want your head to be hitting something that is inflating that fast.

The passenger's head ideally hits the airbag as it is deflating, not inflating. If you were to hit a fully inflated basketball with your fist, it would hurt. But if you hit a deflating basketball, then your fist would bounce back and it wouldn't hurt as much. That's what you want your head to do—bounce back from the deflating airbag.

That's why timing is everything! It is not only important that the airbag inflates immediately, but also crucial that it deflates just as quickly, so that it will provide a good cushion instead of a firm surface.

# Sensing an Accident

How does an airbag know when to deploy? The airbag control unit (ACU) detects an impact, evaluates it, and instantaneously begins necessary safety measures, usually starting the chain reaction that inflates the airbag. It may also provide tension to the seat belts, pulling them tight.

The ACU is connected to sensors installed throughout the car. Those sensors are tuned to watch for abrupt changes in acceleration and respond appropriately. The number of sensors inside each car varies, depending on the manufacturer. A more fully automated car may have up to thirty.

The ACU acts differently, depending on the type of accident.

- Following a frontal impact, a sensor interprets the resulting vibrations as a crash and sends a signal to the airbag to inflate. These types of sensors are called micro-mechanical oscillators.
- In a rollover, a micro-mechanical gyroscope registers the rotation of the vehicle and triggers the seat belts to tighten and the airbags to deploy.

Have you ever been in a car when the driver slams on the brakes? If so, after you were propelled forward, you probably felt the seat belt tighten across your chest, pulling you back into your seat. The sensors read the situation and told the seat belt to stop you from flying forward. Having an ACU is like having your own miniengineer, right inside your car.

How does this miniengineer deploy the ACU?

1. When an impact is detected, a mechanical switch is flipped inside the sensor.
2. This closes an electrical circuit and sends a signal to the ACU.
3. The ACU then sends an ignition signal to the airbag, which sets off the chemical reaction that causes it to inflate.

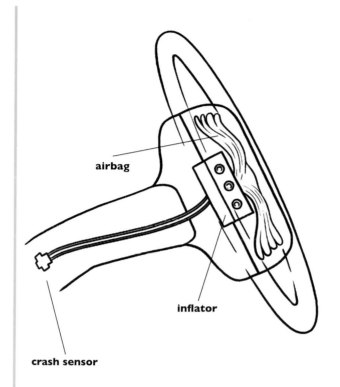

*Diagram of a steering wheel containing an uninflated airbag, inflator, and crash sensor*

# Advantages of Airbags

An airbag can save your life, or at the very least, hopefully lessen your injuries. Sounds like a great invention. Would you believe that this safety feature almost didn't make it into cars?

Airbags have saved a lot of lives, but they've also caused a lot of injuries, and some deaths. It's your turn. You are the engineer. Take a look at the advantages and disadvantages of airbags.

Airbags provide the following benefits:
- preventing the driver from hitting the steering wheel
- preventing the passenger from hitting the dashboard
- preventing all passengers from hitting doors and/or the roof
- minimizing injuries
- keeping passengers inside the vehicle

**Airbags do not deploy if a car is in reverse. Some cars include rear-curtain airbags that deploy behind backseat passengers if the car is rear-ended.**

# Disadvantages of Airbags

Airbags have a number of shortcomings.
- An airbag only deploys when a collision equal to the force of a car hitting a brick wall at between 10 and 15 mph (16 to 24 kph) takes place.
- Sometimes the force of an impact is not enough for an airbag to deploy.
- Sometimes an airbag just fails to deploy for mechanical reasons.
- An airbag can deploy when it shouldn't; occasionally, one may deploy when a car hits a big bump in the road.
- An airbag will also deploy if a car goes faster than 200 mph (322 kph).
- Even if it successfully deploys, an airbag may cause secondary injuries. Because they deploy at very fast speeds, airbags can cause broken bones or bruises.
- In very rare cases, passengers can be burned as a result of the high temperature of the chemical reaction.

Some extra words of caution:
- Passengers need to be at least 12 to 18 inches (30 to 46 centimeters) away from an airbag to avoid being hurt by the force of deployment.
- Front seat passengers under a certain weight can be injured by a deploying airbag. That's why children under the age of twelve shouldn't sit in the front seat.

What would you to do fix the problems that happen with an airbag? Do you think the advantages outweigh the disadvantages?

# Meet Some New Members of the Family

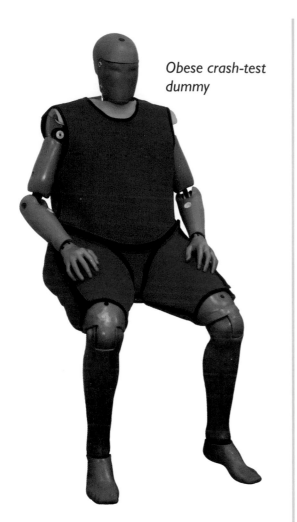

*Obese crash-test dummy*

In order to get the most accurate information available, a crash-test dummy must mimic the size and shape of an actual person. In the 1980s, crash-test dummies were built to match the average male human height and weight at the time.

That approach left out drivers who didn't fit that average size standard and ignored women altogether. Moreover, in the next few decades, humans grew heavier on average, and many elderly people continued to drive. Engineers have to take these changes into consideration in order to design safety features that will protect more people.

How do engineers figure out how adjust the design of crash-test dummies? The best way is to consult with doctors who treat accident victims. An emergency room doctor is likely to see a lot of different people who have been in all sorts of crashes.

In January of 2017, engineers at Humanetics, one of the leading manufacturers of crash-test dummies, teamed up with Stewart Wang, a trauma surgeon at the University of Michigan, to design new dummies.

Wang reported that many of his patients were heavier, which had a big effect on the types of injuries they received. He observed that obese people had twice as many injuries to the lower part of their bodies as a people of average weight. That is mainly because during an impact, an obese person may "submarine," or slide down under the seat belt.

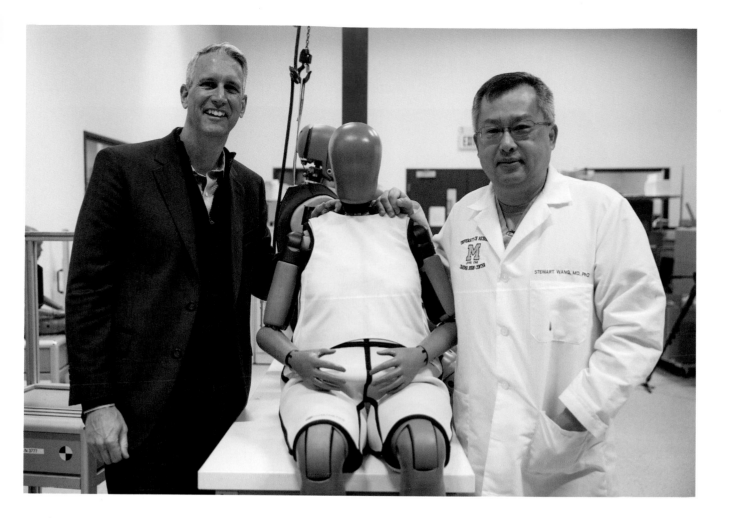

*Christopher J. O'Connor of Humanetics and Stewart Wang with an elderly ATD*

Elderly people often suffer different types of injuries. For one thing, their bones may be more brittle and may break more easily. Also, as a person gets older, the spine can curve, causing the chest to sag. Because of this, older people are also fifteen times as likely to have severe chest injuries. Chest injuries in older patients are very serious and often fatal.

In consultation with Wang, Humanetics created two new crash-test dummies: one that weighs 273 pounds (124 kilograms) and one that is based on an overweight seventy-year-old woman.

# Putting on the Paint

*A technician applies greasepaint before a crash test*

Crash-test dummies require some snazzy styling. They've got to be wearing just the right outfit. Passengers will be wearing clothes, after all, and the fabric could cause someone to slide around. Once a dummy's wardrobe is sorted out, it's time to add some make-up.

Engineers need to know exactly which part of a dummy's body hits the airbag. Although tests are recorded, the video doesn't always give an accurate report. So the researchers paint the dummies' body parts with different colors.

During a collision, a driver or passenger may move in several different directions. In a crash test, the paint rubs off the dummy and onto anything it touches. That helps engineers understand how the human body might move during in a crash.

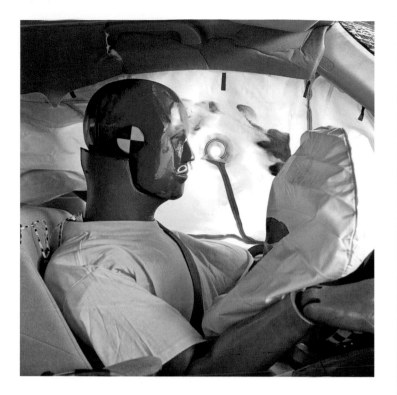

*Greasepaint is transferred from a crash-test dummy's body to parts of the car, allowing engineers to see where the body struck the inside of the car and how the airbags worked.*

# chapter 6

# Look Out Behind You!

Focus. It's the one thing that you absolutely need when you are driving. You need to pay attention to everything that is happening in front of you, to either side, and behind you. With so much going on in and out of the car, a driver must make an almost superhuman effort to stay focused.

# What Do Mirrors Do?

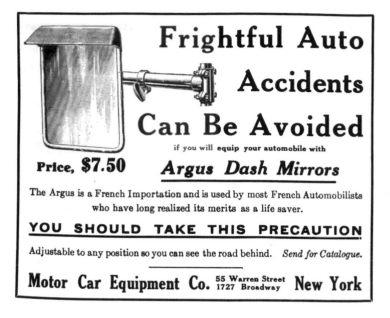
*Ad for the Argus Dash Mirror from* Cycle and Automobile Trade Journal, *Volume 13, October 1, 1908*

Drivers must routinely swivel their head to keep a close eye on what's going on around their cars. Thankfully, they have mirrors to help.

The rearview mirror shows what's directly behind the car. Side-view mirrors help you to see what's happening on either side of the car.

Rearview mirrors are not a recent development. The first ones were found on buggies pulled by horses. After all, a driver needed to know if another horse and buggy was about to overtake him.

The Argus Dash Mirror is believed to have been the first automotive rearview mirror. Created in France in 1908, it was mounted on the driver's side of the car and could be tilted to the proper angle.

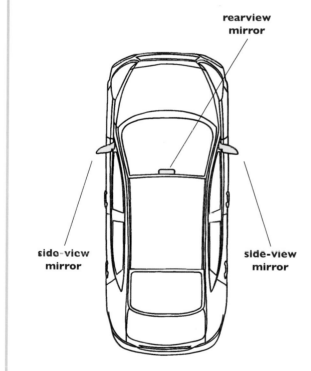

*Location of mirrors on a car*

*Photograph of Dorothy Levitt from*
The Woman and the Car

*Dorothy Levitt driving a Napier at Brighton July 1905*

*Story about Dorothy Levitt from*
Los Angeles Herald,
*January 06, 1907*

In 1909, British racing driver Dorothy Levitt recommended using a rearview mirror in her book *The Woman and the Car: A Chatty Little Handbook for the Edwardian Motoriste*. Levitt suggested that all women "carry a little hand-mirror in a convenient place when driving" so they could "hold the mirror aloft from time to time in order to see behind while driving in traffic."

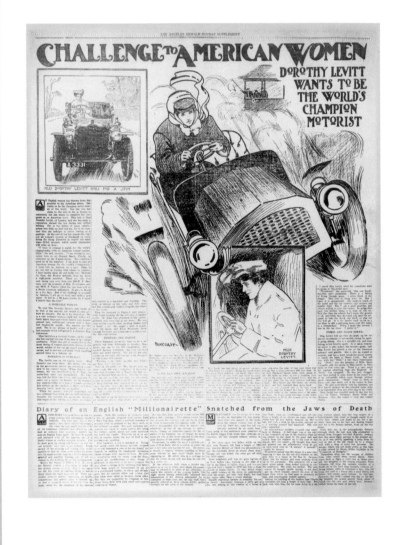

It wasn't until 1911 that the benefits of the rearview mirror became well-known. That was the year when race car driver Ray Harroun added one to the Marmon Wasp that he drove in the very first Indianapolis 500 race. Harroun used the mirror instead of carrying a passenger as his "spotter," as had been the custom. It was pretty controversial at the time. How did it work out? Harroun won the race! And people began to take note of the rearview mirror.

*Ray Harroun in his Marmon Wasp Driven by in the first Indianapolis 500*

Haroun won the first Indianapolis 500 in 6 hours, 42 minutes, and 8 seconds. His average speed was 74.6 mph (120 kph). Today's Indy 500 drivers average between 165 and 185 mph (266 and 298 kph) and can finish the race in just over 2 hours.

# Rearview Mirrors

*Ad for the Cop-Spotter*

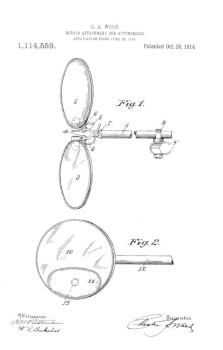

*Diagram from Chester A. Weed's patent for a rearview mirror*

Still, the rearview mirror wasn't seen on a lot of cars until about 1921. That's when Elmer Berger, an electrical engineer, created a standard sized mirror that could be bought as an accessory and added to any model car. Many people started buying Berger's mirrors.

For safety? Perhaps. Or, more likely, because he called it a "Cop-Spotter." Berger told people that if they used his rearview mirror, they were less likely to be pulled over by a policeman for speeding. Berger filed two applications, but he never received a patent nor any money for the rearview mirrors that were later mass-produced.

Berger wasn't the only rearview mirror inventor whose efforts were thwarted. In 1914, Chester A. Weed received a patent for a mirror that helped drivers get a full rear view of the road. He never received any money either.

By the 1930s, car companies had created their own rearview mirrors. They were usually installed inside the vehicle in the middle of the upper portion of the windshield. This gave the driver the best, and widest, view, of the road behind the car. They were easy and safer to use, because the driver didn't have to take his eyes off the road to turn to look behind him; instead he could just glance in the mirror. Even with all of the benefits, it wasn't until the 1970s that a rearview mirror became a standard part of a car.

# Side-view Mirrors

During the 1940s and 1950s, most roads were only two lanes wide. The rearview mirrors available at that time did a great job. But by the late 1960s, there were more cars on the road and many highways had more than two lanes. That meant that a driver also needed to see what was happening on either side of the car, as well as behind it. Enter the side-view mirror.

Also known as a wing mirror, fender mirror, or outdoor rearview mirror, the side-view mirror was fastened to the driver's door, near the front windshield. It was also adjustable. The driver could maneuver the mirror so that she could see the lane next to her. It also gave her a different, and more comprehensive, view behind the car.

At first, side-view mirrors were available only on the driver's side. Later, researchers discovered that having a side-view mirror on each side of the car was helpful. After all, if you were in the left lane, it was good to know if a car was to the right of you.

There's gotta be better way!

# Warning—Backing Up!

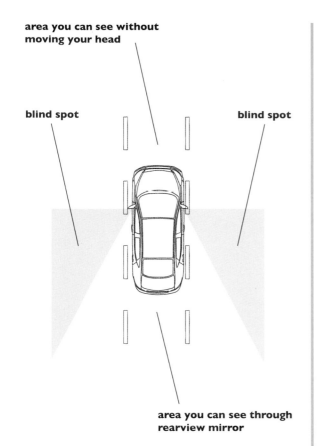

area you can see without moving your head

blind spot

blind spot

area you can see through rearview mirror

Even with three mirrors, each pointed in a different direction, there is still an area behind the car that the driver just can't see. It's called the blind spot. Every car has a blind spot. Its size is related to the height of the driver. Shorter people have bigger blind spots. That is because they must adjust the angle of the mirror, which reduces the area of visibility behind them.

Unfortunately, the blind spot can be just the right size to hide another car. Accidents can and do happen when a driver tries to change lanes and hits another car in the blind spot.

Car design also affects the blind spot. Cars manufactured in the 1970s and 1980s were boxy and long. They also had large rear windows that provided an unobstructed view—little to no blind spot. What changed?

Those big cars were gas guzzlers. Oh, and they were also unsafe in many ways. The big windshields provided a good view, but these cars didn't have reinforced roofs and crumple zones. Surviving a major accident without injury was practically impossible. Car companies decided to correct some of these flaws in future cars by incorporating stronger roofs and headrests to their new models. But adding these safety features often increased the size of the driver's blind spot.

- In order to reinforce the roof, the rear windshield had to be smaller.
- To prevent whiplash, engineers added headrests to the front seats, but they obstructed the driver's view.
- Larger bumpers made it more difficult for the driver to see the road behind the car.

The result was more collisions from drivers backing into something…or unfortunately, some one.

# "Closer Than They Appear"

In 2012, R. Andrew Hicks, a Drexel University math professor, came up with a brand new side-view mirror. His version allowed the driver to have a much wider range of vision behind him. The secret?

Hicks's mirror was curved. Flat mirrors only allow the driver to see about 15 to 17 degrees of the area behind the car. Hicks's curved mirror allowed the driver to see up to 45 degrees.

Imagine a large pizza cut into eight slices. A circle is 180 degrees, so each slice represents 45 degrees. If you sat in the middle of the pizza and used a normal mirror to look behind you, you could only see half a pizza slice. But if you used Hicks's mirror, you could see a whole slice.

While a curved mirror shows you a wider view, that view is distorted. A flat mirror gives the driver a more accurate sense of the actual distance between the car and other objects. This has to do with the way the image is reflected in the mirror. As a result, the National Highway Transportation Safety Administration would not allow Hicks's mirror to be used.

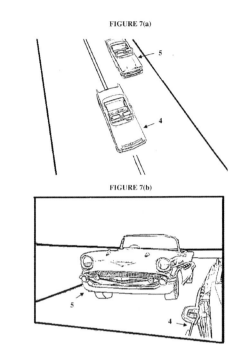

FIGURE 7(a)

FIGURE 7(b)

*Diagram from R. Andrew Hicks's patent for "wide angle substantially non-distorting mirror"*

*Above: Hicks's mirror*
*Below: standard side-view mirror*

A curved mirror is called a convex mirror. This means the mirror bulges slightly toward you, giving you a different angle of vision.

# The Rise of the Rearview Camera

*1956 Buick Centurion*

If only there was a piece of equipment that would allow the driver to see the entire area behind the car. It would have to be small, and it couldn't obstruct the driver's view. And it would have to provide immediate information, so the driver could see what was actually happening in real time. Ideally, its use would not be influenced by the height of the driver. What could it be?

It is a video camera. With its wide-angle lens, this kind of camera can show everything behind a car.

The very first rearview or backup camera was used in the 1956 Buick Centurion Dream Car. This car was way ahead of its time, technologically speaking. The front seats automatically slid back when a door was opened, to allow for easy entrance. The rocket-inspired body had long swooping tail fins and a glass-topped roof. (Probably not very safe in a rollover.) Still, the red leather seats, fancy steering wheel, and rocket-shaped taillights probably made the driver feel like he was steering a plane instead of a car.

And there was a camera mounted on the hood, instead of any rear- or side-view mirrors. The camera sent images to a four-inch by six-inch (ten-centimeter by fifteen-centimeter) cathode ray television screen located in the dashboard.

Created by Harley Earl and Charles Jordan, the Centurion was intended to be displayed in the General Motors Motorama traveling show, where car designs of the future were exhibited. The car was never put into production, most likely because it would have been extremely expensive to make.

Still, the idea of using a rearview camera was a good one. The problem was the expense. And the technology. Before the 1990s, cameras were large and bulky. They stuck out and made the car look weird.

In 1991, Toyota experimented with a new version. They created a rearview camera for the Soarer Limited. It turned on when the car gearshift was put into reverse. This car was never sold in the United States.

The first car to be sold in the United States with a rearview camera was the Infiniti Q60. Infiniti called their camera a "rear monitor." It worked the same way as the Toyota camera. When the driver put the car into reverse, an image of the area behind the car appeared on the screen.

The backup camera located on the rear of the 1956 Buick Centurion

Monitor in the dashboard of an Infiniti Q60

# Recording Every Move

The rearview camera is engaged when the car is put into reverse. It transmits images to a screen on the dashboard or to a tiny frame within the rearview mirror, originally via wires that run under the car. More recent versions use wireless technology to connect the camera and monitor.

Some monitors include lines on the screen that indicate distance. This allows the driver to know how far he is away from something. The lines may be colored like a stoplight:

- red for the closest objects
- yellow for near objects
- green for distant objects

Once cameras became popular additions to cars, it only seemed natural to use the "extra set of eyes" to help with other driving functions. Today some cars have as many as ten cameras set all around the car, providing full 360-degree visibility. They help with keeping you in your lane, maintaining the distance between you and the car in front of you, and even parallel parking.

By May 2018, NHTSA required all new cars to be equipped with rearview cameras. They must cover a 10 x 20 foot (3 x 6 meter) area behind the car.

*Driver's view of the image from a rearview camera with a person behind the vehicle*

# What Does a Rearview Camera Show?

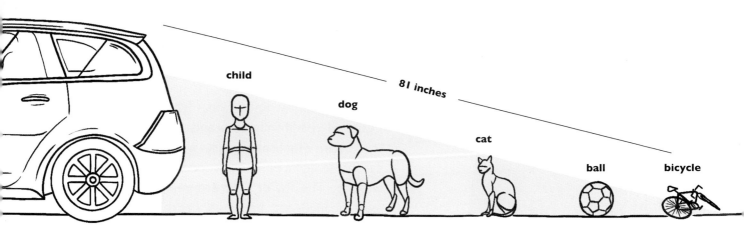

A good rearview camera covers an area up to 81 inches (206 centimeters) behind the car. It is usually mounted on or near the trunk handle or license plate. As a result, it has a much lower perspective than the driver and that eliminates much of the blind spot.

According to NHSTA, approximately 210 people are killed and 15,000 injured every year as a result of back-over accidents.

# Meet the Pedestrian Crash-test Dummy

*Hybrid III Pedestrian*

Pedestrians are unpredictable. Sometimes they walk out in front of cars, either because they don't see them coming or they assume they'll stop. So safety engineers designed a crash-test dummy that has been programmed to "walk.". The driver must slam on the brakes to avoid hitting it.

This dummy, known as Hybrid III Pedestrian, was designed specifically to stand up. It has a much stiffer low back, which allows for a curved spine. Its knees can be straight or bent, in order to simulate a person walking. The lower legs are replaceable, to allow for easy change-out between crashes. Best of all, this dummy can stand up all by itself. Like the other crash-test dummies, it is available in various sizes and weights.

Most state laws say that as long as you can use two of the three mirrors, you can drive your car. But be careful. Police can still pull you over and possibly even give you a ticket for not having all your mirrors intact.

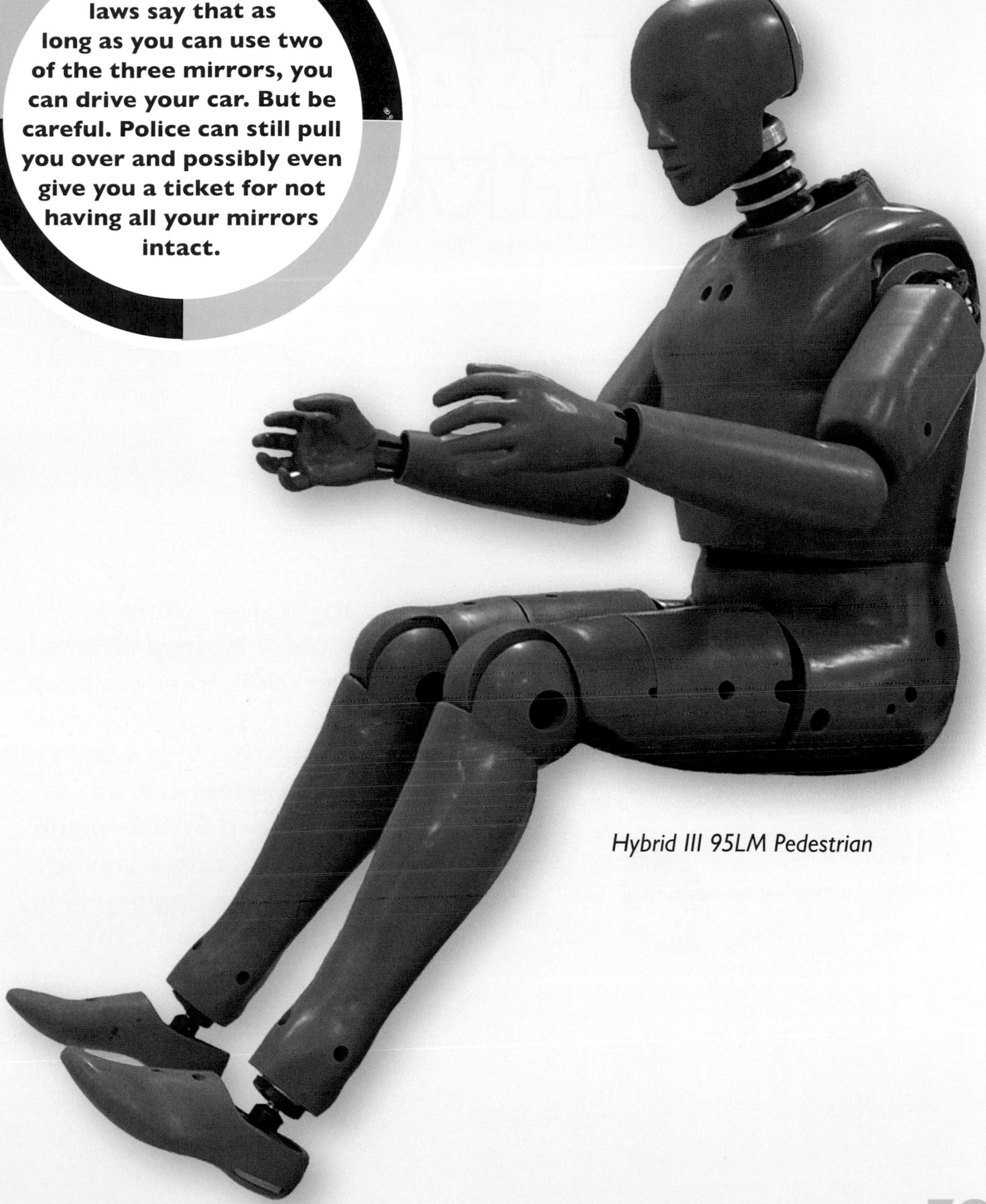

*Hybrid III 95LM Pedestrian*

79

# chapter 7

# Robot Drivers

Right now, there are almost twenty different car companies working to create an autonomous, or self-driving, car. While a driverless car was once only seen in late-night science fiction movies, possibly being driven by a crazed robot, that is no longer the case.

# What Does a Self-driving Car Do?

*1950s illustration featuring the self-driving car of the future*

Self-driving cars can

- park themselves,
- maintain their lanes,
- stay a safe distance from the car in front of them, and
- brake to avoid hitting anything.

With all that in a car, why do you need a human driver? Many car companies say you don't. Just sit back, relax, and ride. Sounds easy, doesn't it?

# Tailgating Is a Necessity

*The American Wonder, featured in* Electronic World *magazine 1925*

The very first self-driving car was created in 1925. This prototype, developed by Houdina Radio Control Company, was the only one of its kind. Called the American Wonder or the Phantom Auto, it was directed by a remote-control radio operated by a person in another car directly behind it. In this case, tailgating was encouraged. The cars had to stay close to one another because the transmitters needed to be within several hundred feet of each other.

How did this newfangled car go over? Not great. It was bulky and moved slowly, and—let's face it—it was weird to have another car following that close. Still, it did make headlines, in part because the first self driving car was also the first self-driving car to crash.

On July 28, 1925, the American Wonder traveled down Broadway, in New York City, just missing a fire engine, two trucks, and a milk wagon, before slamming into a car carrying several men who were filming.

# The Safe Highway of Tomorrow

*GM Firebird II*

In the 1950s, the self-driving car took a new turn. Sensors were embedded in the roads instead of in the cars. If people couldn't drive safely, then engineers would make the road as safe as possible for people.

Sensors in an electric cable in the road would send electronic signals to a car when it was getting too close to the edge or to the lane line. The sensors could also detect the position and speed of other cars on the road and transmit the information to the self-driving car.

This was an extremely expensive idea. It involved placing sensors at regular distances along long stretches of road. In fact, it took over two-and-a-half years for the first cable to be laid on a 400-foot (123 meter) section.

This system also limited the self-driving car to roads where these sensors had been installed. What if you needed to go to the store, but the only road you could take didn't have sensors?

Not surprisingly, this car, known as the GM Firebird II, was never mass-produced, but it did make a big splash at the Motorama car show of 1956.

# The Rise of the Robot Driver

*Exterior and interior of VaMoRs*

It would be another fifty years until engineers had more success with self-driving cars. In 1986, Mercedes-Benz developed the first true autonomous car. German professor Ernst Dickmanns reengineered a van so that a computer controlled the braking, steering, and throttle. Four cameras on each side of the vehicle transmitted information to the computer. Dickmanns successfully drove his van thousands of miles through traffic, sometimes at speeds of over 110 mph (177 kph). This van, dubbed VaMoRs, was a success! And yet, it would still be many more years before self-driving cars would become a more easily accessible technology, and even longer before it would be affordable.

# DARPA in the Desert

*Sandstorm at the 2004 DARPA Grand Challenge*

How did we get from the 1980s autonomous car to the self-driving vehicles of today? A contest.

In 2002, the United States Defense Advanced Research Projects Administration (DARPA) challenged engineers to come up with a working self-driving vehicle. The prize? One million dollars.

Engineers around the world got to work. More than one hundred teams registered for the first DARPA Grand Challenge in 2004, but none of the vehicles entered in the race were able to complete the 150-mile (240 kilometer) course through the Mojave Desert. Sandstorm, the car created by a team from Carnegie-Mellon University got the farthest—7.32 miles (11.78 kilometers).

By 2007, six teams were able to finish the course. The technology developed as a result of these contests has contributed significantly to the production of the self-driving cars being tested today.

# Engineering a Self-driving Car

Google co-founder Sergey Brin shows US Secretary of State John Kerry the sensor displays inside a Google's self-driving car, 2016.

In order to operate, a self-driving car must know

- where it is,
- where it is going, and
- how it can get there safely.

To achieve this, the car must be able to do these three main tasks on its own:

1. sense its surroundings,
2. process the information by modeling and making decisions, and
3. react with appropriate movement.

Engineers must work on each of these tasks individually, using the method of deduction. Then the three tasks are put together and tested. They are evaluated, adjusted, retested, and evaluated again until all the pieces work together.

# Where Am I?

Self-driving cars rely upon many systems to figure out where they are on the road. A Light Detection and Ranging (LIDAR) sensor is a camera that has between thirty-two and sixty different lasers. Each laser beam bounces off of an individual object and records its distance from the car. The sensor compiles all of this information simultaneously and creates a 3-D map of everything near the car—stoplights, trees, other cars, or even human beings.

How far the LIDAR can see depends on how good the individual system is. Some systems can see up to 656 feet (200 meters); others can see down to a few centimeters, but only as far as 328 feet (100 meters) from the car.

Each self-driving car has many other sensors, including

- bumper-mounted radar,
- a regular camera at driver height to "see" as a human driver would, and
- sensors that monitor the wheels.

All of these sensors are usually mounted on the outside of the car. Inside the car, there are other sensors, such as

- an altimeter to tell the car how high it is off the ground (so it can sense if it has crashed or gone off the road);
- a gyroscope to keep the car on track, or moving in a straight line down the road; and
- a tachometer to measure how fast the engine is revving, or how fast the car is going.

# Where Am I Going?

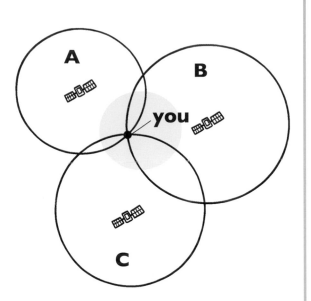

*Diagram of trilateration*

**The 1995 Oldsmobile 88 was the first commercially available car with GPS installed. That added more than $2000 (the equivalent of more than $3,200 in 2018) to the price of the car. And it wasn't even that accurate.**

When you get into a car, you have to know where you are going. Back in the old days, that meant using a paper map. Ideally, a passenger was designated the navigator—the one who guided the driver. It was the navigator's job to unfold the massive, newspaper-size map and identify the best route to take. One of the navigator's most difficult jobs was anticipating a turn before the driver missed it.

In the early 2000s, all of that changed.

Not long after the Global Positioning System (GPS) hit the scene, piles of paper maps ended up in the recycling bin. GPS was digital. Now you could figure out where you were going by looking at a map on a screen.

GPS is made up of twenty-four different satellites that are orbiting the Earth about 125 miles (20,000 kilometers) overhead. Each satellite transmits its position and time in regular intervals. The GPS receiver in your car or cellphone intercepts (or receives) these signals. Once it has accurate time and position information from three different satellites, it can tell you where you are.

Why three? Three is the minimum number of satellites for an accurate position, using a system called "trilateration." A circle is drawn around the point of your location from each satellite. The place where the three circles intersect is your location. For example, if you are close to satellite A, you will be in the upper left circle. The upper right circle indicates how far you are from satellite B, and the bottom circle does the same for satellite C.

# The Brains of the Car

The Electronic Control Unit (ECU) is the "brains" of the self-driving car. An ECU is a tiny digital computer that reads signals sent by sensors throughout the car. But there isn't just one ECU per car—there are hundreds.

ECU sensors monitor all of this and more:

speed
braking
cruise control
traction
tire pressure
fuel level
transmission
emissions
lighting
windshield wipers
climate control
airbags
seat belts
security
navigation
entertainment

Each ECU is in charge of monitoring a particular system and is programmed to react based on the information it receives from that system. For example, if the sensor indicates that the car engine temperature is too high, the ECU will turn on the check engine light. This lets the "driver" know there is a problem.

The main "brain" of a self-driving car is usually one computer, which receives all of the information from every sensor and ECU in the car. Each company designs its own software, so the systems can be different. Many researchers are experimenting with artificial intelligence—computers that can think for themselves and learn from their mistakes, something that human drivers ideally already know how to do.

ECUs can be hacked. In 2015, two hackers took over a Jeep Cherokee and caused the transmission to shut down on a highway. Fortunately, no one was hurt

# Advantages of Self-driving Cars

Got books? A company named Harman has designed Σtos, a self-driving car featuring its very own bookshelf!

A robot driver is safer than a human one. Well, at least that's what the car companies who are creating self-driving cars say.

Some statistics support that claim. According to the Centers for Disease Control and Prevention, over 33,000 people died in car accidents in 2015. Most of those deaths might have been preventable. What causes many car accidents? Distracted drivers, who are on their phones, dealing with their kids, changing the music, or just feeling sleepy.

A robot driver is never distracted. It can drive for many hours without ever needing sleep, food, or even a bathroom break. While the robot is driving, you can just sit back and chat, play a video game, or read a book!

# Disadvantages of Self-driving Cars

Self-driving cars will bring about huge changes, and there are many unanswered questions about their use on public roadways. If a self-driving car gets into an accident, who is responsible?

- Can you sue a robot driver?
- Will the human passenger have to pay?
- Will the car manufacturer have to pay?

Questions such as these will need to be resolved before self-driving cars can hit the roads. There are also some engineering issues that still need to be addressed—things that most human drivers understand or are familiar with.

- **Precipitation**: Some sensors have a hard time figuring out if it is raining or snowing. They don't sense the difference, so they can't make the necessary adjustment for driving on a wet or icy road.
- **Unusual circumstances**: What if a stoplight is out? Self-driving cars may not understand how to respond. And more importantly, they will not know how to follow a police officer's hand signals.
- **Obstructions**: Construction areas can also be challenging for self-driving cars. They aren't quite sure what to do with obstructions on the road. Sometimes drivers have to follow detours or unusual paths that are marked off with traffic cones. A self-driving car may just ignore the cones and drive right through.

Finally, there are the humans themselves. Sometimes people will walk out right in front of a car. Or, if a pedestrian sees a driver coming, she might signal that she is about to walk out, assuming that the driver will slow down.

According to Google, self-driving cars have been involved in over 12 crashes—and human error was to blame in every one.

# The Digital Dummy

With all of the new technology in the self-driving car, will there still be a need for crash-test dummies? Yes, but that has always been the case. The crash-test dummies need to keep evolving.

The current models don't have enough high-tech sensors to record all the information that engineers need to know about a self-driving car accident. So right now, the "dummy" inside a self-driving car…is a human.

While autonomous cars are still in development, a human must be inside each vehicle during testing. After all, if the car starts to swerve into another lane, or fails to slow down as it approaches another car, a dummy is no help. A human needs to take control.

Almost all self-driving cars are equipped with a way to disengage the computer and allow the human ddriver to take over. Fortunately, the self-driving cars haven't crashed very often, so the human passengers are usually safe.

New car technology has also given rise to a new type of crash-test dummy. Meet the new digital dummy, or, as they are being called, "crash-test avatars". This type of test takes place entirely on computers. An avatar of a human being is created based on actual scans of a person. The scans are done by magnetic resonance imaging (MRI) and computerized tomography (CT or CAT scan), and the information is read into a computer. Using that information, researchers create an avatar of that exact size and weight and place it into a specific car. The car is then sent down a road with specific conditions and crashed into an object. Readings are taken from the avatar and computed to show the damage the human would have received. All of this is done on a computer. No more spending $30,000 to have an actual car containing a crash-test dummy slam into a solid object.

# The Crash-test Cyclist

*The crash-test cyclist at work*

Not all crash-test dummies are going away. Meet the crash-test cyclist. Talk about a balancing act! Designed by Toyota, this ATD rides a bike down the road next to a self-driving car. The idea is to teach the car how to interact with a bicyclist. Bicyclists are unpredictable. They can weave between cars, or pop out in unexpected places on the road. A self-driving car computer has a hard time figuring them out. Toyota felt that if their car had to deal with one, they'd better be safe and make crash-test dummies. Not surprisingly, none of their human engineers had volunteered for the job.

# Driving the Future

*Ehang 184 passenger drone*

Where will self-driving cars take us in the future? If Waymo has its way, there will be a time when you can use an app on your phone to call for a self-driving car just like you can call for a normal car with a driver now. There might be self-driving race cars, taxis, buses, and delivery trucks, as well as cars. Some experts believe that in ten years, self-driving cars will be everywhere. Elon Musk, the head of Tesla Motors, has predicted that driverless cars will be seen on more roads as early as 2020. It depends, of course, on where you live. It is most likely that would happen in the states that have already set up laws for driverless cars.

Excited about the future? Can't wait to check out an autonomous ride? Here are a few of the self-driving cars on the roads right now:

- self-driving bus in Las Vegas, NV
  *www.fortune.com/2017/01/14/vegas-self-driving-bus*
- self-driving Uber car in Pittsburgh, PA
  *www.wired.com/2016/09/self-driving-autonomous-uber-pittsburgh*
- driverless trams in cities in Greece, Switzerland, the UK, China, and the Netherlands
  *www.gizmodo.com.au/2015/10/5-cities-with-driverless-public-buses-on-the-streets-right-now*

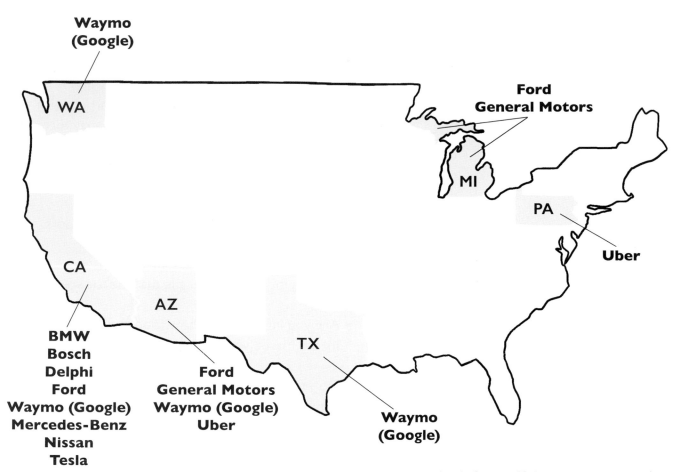

**Waymo (Google)**

**WA**

**Ford General Motors**

**MI**

**PA**

**Uber**

**CA**

**AZ**

**TX**

**BMW**
**Bosch**
**Delphi**
**Ford**
**Waymo (Google)**
**Mercedes-Benz**
**Nissan**
**Tesla**

**Ford**
**General Motors**
**Waymo (Google)**
**Uber**

**Waymo (Google)**

*Look for a self-driving car near you!*

And what about flying cars? Are they the next "new" technology? Maybe. Check out the eHang 184, an autonomous airplane introduced at the 2016 Consumer Electronics Show. It is a fully functioning sky car for one person. It looks sort of like a helicopter but with four whirling blades—a quadcopter. The eHang is built for just one passenger. Maybe you'll have a chance to get your own pilot's license one day.

Who will win the race to get the first self-driving car widely available to the public? No one knows. But there is one thing that you can count on: the self-driving car will not only make driving safer for humans, it will also save the "lives" of many crash-test dummies.

# So You Want to Be an Engineer?

Engineering is the part of science concerned with the design, building, and use of machines, structures, or engines. It's also really cool!

Most people who become engineers have lots of questions about the world. They want to know how things work. Are you like that?

There are several different kinds of engineers.

- Want to design planes or rocket ships? Aeronautical engineering is the one for you.

- Are you interested in how food and drugs are made? Maybe you'd like to be a chemical engineer.

- Do you want to know how to construct a building to withstand an earthquake? You might be interested in civil engineering.

- Ever wonder how computers or robotics work? Consider studying computer or electrical engineering.

- Do you like to tinker with machines to see how they work? You could be a mechanical engineer.

- Are you interested in finding ways to make oil and gas extraction more efficient and eco-friendly? Maybe you'd like to be a petroleum engineer

Whatever type of engineering interests you, remember this: engineers provide the link between scientific discoveries and commercial application. What does that mean? Computer scientists figured out how to create all of the systems that are used in a self-driving car, but it's the engineers who helped apply that knowledge to building the actual car that can drive itself!

Being an engineer means developing great problem-solving techniques. It also encourages people to learn from failure. Yep. That's right. Failing at something is acceptable in engineering because it teaches you that that design is incorrect, which leads you to problem-solve how to correct it.

Think about Crash and his fellow crash-test dummies. Their very existence is owed to the idea of failure. They are the ones who get to endure the bumps, scrapes, and yes, even occasional dismemberments as the engineer's tweak and perfect their design. Thank goodness we have them!

Will the use of self-driving cars lead to the end of Crash and his friends? Not likely. Engineers are also great inventors! They are always looking ahead to the next project.

Take a look at some of the ways we may travel in the future:

**Hyperloop:** Could you travel to work or school via an overhead track? Probably best if you're not afraid of heights!

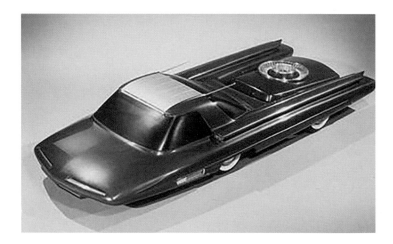

**Nuclear-powered cars:** The 1958 Ford Nucleon concept car was a scale model. A small nuclear reactor in the back of the vehicle would generate power for a steam engine. At the time, nuclear reactors were too big to fit into cars, so none were ever made. But, with today's technology and the use of thorium, you never know.

**Martin Jetpack:** How would you like to fly to school on your own? Maybe some day you will with this jetpack. How cool would that be? The only problem is, where would you store it? It's clearly too big to fit into your locker.

Where will the transportation of the future take us? Flying cars? Spaceships to Mars? Deep beneath the ocean? The possibilities are endless! But one thing is certain: in order to make any of these journeys, we'll need the help of lots of engineers and, of course, the crash-test dummies. #SafetyFirst

# Photo Credits

**Advertising Archive/Everett Collection**
18, 81

**Center for Pet Safety**
14 (crash-test dummy dog)

**Creative Commons**
7, 20 (Richard Smith), 21, 26, 27 (Ford Motor Company), 31 (Kevauto), 38 (Tucker Torpedo, Thomas), 52 (DaimlerChrysler AG), 66 (Johan), 74 (John Lloyd), 75 (Centurion, Eric Kilby; (Infiniti Q60, Amoore100), 80 (Grendelkhan), 83 (Karrmann), 85 (MikeMurphy), 94 (Alex Butterfield), 97

**Delaware Public Archives**
22 (wooden bumper)

**Ernst Dickmanns**
84

**Guy Kilroy**, *www.myguysmoving.com*
8

**The Henry Ford (Gift of Liberty Mutual Insurance Company)**
39 (Cornell-Liberty Safety Car)

**R. Andrew Hicks / Sophie Hicks**
73 (mirror photo)

**Humanetics Innovative Solutions, Inc.**
14 (Hybrid III and Hybrid III 5%), 29, 62–63, 78–79

**Insurance Institute for Highway Safety**
64–65

**Library of Congress**
68 (*Los Angeles Herald*, January 6, 1907, Image 40)

**Los Angeles Times**
23 (*Los Angeles Herald*)

**Mechanix Illustrated**
39 (Sir Vival car)

**Nationaal Archief / Spaarnestad Photo / Het Leven**
19

**National Highway Transportation Safety Administration**
50–51

**public domain**
12 (1961 Corporate Annual Report), 13 (Dynamic Test Center, AGU Zürich), 16, 17, 25, 32 (National Institute of Standards and Technology and Technology Automobile Research collection), 34, 37, 44, 46 (Automobilia-L'Automobile aux Armées), 47, 54, 55, 58 (Lupin, Arpingstone), 67, 68 (Levitt photographs), 69, 70, 73 (Hicks patent), 82

**Rinspeed**
90

**Andy Saunders**
22 (Aurora)

**Toyota's Collaborative Safety Research Center**
93

**United States Air Force / Keith Wright**
76

**United States Department of Transportation**
15

**United States Department of State**
86

**Volvo Car Group**
40

# Index